The Rough Side of the Mountain

The Rough Side of the Mountain

Black Women's Ministries in Unitarian Universalism

EDITED BY QIYAMAH A. RAHMAN

Skinner House Books
Boston

Copyright © 2022 by Qiyamah A. Rahman. All rights reserved. Published by Skinner House Books, an imprint of the Unitarian Universalist Association, 24 Farnsworth St., Boston, MA 02210–1409.

www.skinnerhouse.org

Printed in the United States

Text design by Tim Holtz
Cover design by Kaleema Al-Nur

print ISBN: 978-1-55896-892-9
eBook ISBN: 978-1-55896-893-6

6 5 4 3 2 1
26 25 24 23 22

CIP on file with the Library of Congress.

Contents

MINISTERIAL JOURNEYS AND REFLECTIONS

POETRY

The Dead Do Not Remain Dead
DEDICATED TO OUR SISTA MINISTERS

They surface among us
the memories sometimes overpowering
memories of their smiles, their looks when vexed,
their acts of kindness in the streets, on the subways, at the
    capital on a march, on the chancel—wisdom words
    flowing.
The power of their words soothed us and comfort us still.
We cannot forget you.
We treasure the stories that tell of your kindness, your
    bravery, your beauty, your witness and love of life,
    family, friends, and Unitarian Universalism.
You prevailed until your last breath
and like you we will prevail
and speak your names among the living
knowing,
as long as your names are spoken and written,
you live on in our hearts.
We speak your names sista clergy
sista ministers
sista teachers.
We are grateful to you our sistas that you passed this way,
that you shared your lives and your presence for a time.
Rest in Power!
Rest in Peace!

                      —Rev. Dr. Qiyamah A. Rahman

Will there ever be a time when we can authentically be who we are, believe what we believe, speak our own truth, sing our own song—and be with one another?

—**Rev. Rosemary Bray McNatt**

To not be a barrier,
you have to be always assessing the barriers.

—**Paula Cole Jones**

Foreword

The women who have contributed to this volume tell of their faith journeys, journeys that led them into, and sometimes out of, Unitarian Universalism; nurtured commitments to justice; inspired innovative organizations; and guided them onto new paths of study. Each woman is at a different career point, with different experiences of life and motivations to act. Such diversity belies a single view of Black women. In this volume, Black clergy women in the Unitarian Universalist tradition tell stories and share poems that highlight a diversity of life experience but also a commonality, being in the public eye even as they are too often ignored or taken for granted and, therefore, rendered invisible.

That may sound contradictory—both public and invisible. But generally, this contradiction is part of many Black women's lives in the United States. Too often our work is taken for granted. We are sometimes recognized with condescending gratitude and surprise that we achieved something. Yet the truth of our realities has always been that we are accomplished. Recent movies center Black women's unseen lives in history: Harriet, about the famed Underground Railroad conductor, and Hidden Figures, about Black women mathematicians integral to NASA. In 2018, the New York Times began running "overlooked" obituaries of historic Black people. The women included Gladys Bentley (a blues performer who died in 1960), Mary Ellen Pleasant (an abolitionist and millionaire who died in 1907), and Elizabeth Keckly (a formerly enslaved seamstress and friend to Mary Todd Lincoln who died in 1907). These stories have been invisible and represent Black women in a way that many in the United States do not consider normative. Furthering invisibility, women like Oprah or Michelle Obama are held up as exceptions to "normal" Black women, who are viewed as angry welfare queens. Neither stereotype, the exceptional minority nor the social parasite, can begin to represent the diversity of Black women. Black women in less stereotypical roles are ignored—and this includes ministers.

In *The Rough Side of the Mountain*, Black women Unitarian Universalist ministers tell their own truths. And in the process, they are engaged in constructive theological development. Their theological reflections and statements are not theoretical but real, people-centered, self-reflexive, and inclusive. Together, they weave something that can be mislabeled as new only because the artistry of their lives has been too rarely recognized. These authors break new ground, adding to the existing body of knowledge about the lives of religious women, Black faith lives, and engagement with a particular religious tradition.

In a religious tradition that is primarily white, adding to knowledge about Black women's faith lives provides particularly sharp and layered insights, one of which points to the need for the majority members to pay attention. Heeding these truths requires action at a local level. Congregations expect their ministers to listen to them, but when Black women are in leadership, it is necessary to flip the script, to pivot for a different perspective. The only way to achieve true communication is for white members of the congregation to be open to and welcome the views of their Black woman minister.

Here is the bottom line: what is at stake is the dream of Beloved Community. It is not easy. Beloved Community cannot be determined by the loudest voices or a majority. The commitment is to welcome all. To listen. To learn. And then realign expectations to embrace all.

—**Dr. Stephanie Y. Mitchem**
Professor of Religious Studies and Women's and
Gender Studies, University of South Carolina

Preface

This anthology is dedicated to the Black women who have boldly entered Unitarian Universalist ministry despite obstacles, seen and unseen. Undeterred by sexism and racism, they took on the mantle of their calling, claiming and pursuing Beloved Community.

Black UU clergy women, no matter their talent and gifts, have less opportunity to develop and claim their full power and share of recognition than their male colleagues, Black or white. In our white-centered Unitarian Universalist culture, our history is mostly told in a way that explains and validates the world views of white and male clergy. At the same time, we are not told what is missing from those narratives, what the struggles were for Black UU women clergy and other marginalized leaders. That is why I set out to create this book and why it is so important.

I sent out numerous calls to Black UU clergy women for their testimonials. I asked folks to write about their lives, accomplishments, challenges, insights, and reflections on their ministerial formation and journeys, their highs and lows, what brought them to ministry, and what has kept them on the journey, their wisdom, and what broke their hearts. Many were already overextended and others were working on their own projects and could not participate. But some were not even willing to speak with me about their experience in our tradition. And of course, some have died. Where possible, I have included archival material so that we can at least still receive their wisdom and learn of their experience. But even that has been more difficult than I expected. I felt a limitation, blaming myself that I was not working hard enough to uncover Black UU clergy women's narratives. However, in my moments of clarity, I realized the silenced voices were just no longer available to us. Like the breadcrumbs left by Hansel and Gretel and eaten by a bird before the children could follow them back, some Black UU clergy women have had their traces obliterated; they have been rendered invisible, as if they never existed. And some have been so overlooked and wounded by our tradition that participating in a book like this might be traumatic.

Feminist historian Gerda Lerner reminds us of the enormous collective loss inflicted by this erasure and the importance of preserving the voices of marginalized leaders while we still can:

> For every woman whose diary, letters, tracts, or visions survived, there were many others with equal talent and reasoning ability whose records were lost or destroyed. Oppression brings with it the hegemony of the thought and ideas of the dominant culture; thus women's oppression has meant that much of their mental product and creation has been lost forever.[1]

This collection is my response to a moral imperative, a call that was initially planted when I first read Mark Morrison-Reed's book *Black Pioneers in a White Denomination* in 1992. I was inspired by the stories of Black Unitarian, Universalist, and Unitarian Universalist ministers, and I wondered about the stories of Black UU clergy women. So I waited for someone to write about them and to tell their stories. And I waited and waited. Eventually I stopped waiting and wondering. It finally dawned on me that I was the one I had been waiting for. This collection is neither definitive nor comprehensive, but it is both a continuation and a new start.

I hope that in the future our congregations and ministries will be enriched by the increasing leadership of Black transgender and

---

1 Gerda Lerner, *The Creation of Feminist Consciousness: From the Middle Ages to Eighteen-Seventy* (Oxford: Oxford University Press, 1993), 17.

non-binary ministers and that future publications will reflect and amplify that leadership as well. I want to honor the voices of Black clergy who are neither cisgender nor men that are missing from this book, both those I may not have known to invite and those who chose not to be included. The history of our movement has been one of barriers to ministry and harm for trans and nonbinary people, which explains why, as far as we know, the vast majority of non-male Black UU ministers have been cisgender women. This book looks both backward and forward, to what has been and what is not yet, including a time when we have a richer diversity of stories to tell and have created a climate in which all stories are honored.

There is a vacuum of published scholarship on Black UU women and other non-male clergy. I hope this anthology will open minds and inspire others to seek out the stories and history of non-male Black UU ministers, as well as other groups within Unitarian Universalism whose stories have been ignored for too long. The collective consciousnesses of Black people, of women and nonbinary people, of ministers, of Unitarian Universalists, and of all the intersectional identities between these groups will continue to develop out of deep intellectual interrogation, reflection, and collaborative dialogue. It will emerge out of theories not yet created and those theories with no names as we surface, trace, and identify insights and reflections individually and collectively.

Historical Context and Spiritual Roots

Black UU clergy women descend from prophetic women. We are rooted in spiritual heritages and legacies that have produced shamans, healers, mediums, spiritualists, griots, and preacher women for centuries and in cultures around the world. The link between these women from our past and contemporary UU clergy women fighting injustices and working to transform society should never be erased from our stories. We have available to us the legends of women through the generations who have lived their lives in service to a higher calling. For their sacrifices, may we be prompted to remember them and speak their names in our sacred spaces. In African cosmology, our ancestors live on as long as we continue to call on them. In honor and celebration of the prophetic voices that came before, we lift up the divine impulse they inspired in so many.

Africa

While this anthology's focus is primarily contemporary, it is important to recognize the transatlantic connection between Black UU clergy women in the diaspora and women's prophetic leadership through ancient African cultures. However, colonialism has often disrupted and denigrated the history and culture of Indigenous peoples to the extent that the role of women is lost, distorted, or not readily available.

While many ancient African cultures were patriarchal, they nevertheless acknowledged the existence of male and female deities and affirmed the spiritual power, political authority, and social leadership of women.[2] African representations of the sacred feminine reflect the holistic integration of nature and human, divine, and spiritual powers. Some women are called and chosen to carry out significant roles, often during periods of crisis, to provide leadership, to mobilize communities and nations, to protect their lands against invasions, and to heal and bring messages of hope to their people. These women, known by various names in different cultures—mediums, spirit workers, Obeah women, and healers, to name a few—possess a combination of spiritual and warrior qualities. They are often descended from powerful lineages, like Queen Amina of Zazzau (sixteenth century), Queen Nzinga of Ndongo and Matamba (seventeenth century), and Queen Yaa Asantewaa (eighteenth century).

Several prevalent themes inherent in African cosmology and religious practices persisted through slavery and influenced early Black clergy women. These roots, deep and wide, could not be uprooted even by the horrors of enslavement.

Slavery and Christianity

The prophetic voice, according to Marcia Y. Riggs, is confessional, sermonic, political, and poetic.[3] UU theologian Rebecca Parker posits that the "prophetic tradition is aware of suffering and attuned to the brokenness of the world."[4] Some prophetic Black women preachers were not even one generation removed from their African roots and thus knew

---

2   Oyeronke Oyewumi, ed., *African Women and Feminism: Reflecting on the Politics of Sisterhood* (Trenton: Africa World Press, 2004); Simone Schwarz-Bart, Andre Schwarz-Bart, et al., *In Praise of Black Women, Vols. 1–4* (Madison: University of Wisconsin Press, 2001).

3   Marcia Y. Riggs, ed. *Can I Get a Witness?: Prophetic Religious Voices of African American Women: An Anthology.* (Maryknoll: Orbis Books, 1997), xiii.

4   Rebecca Parker and Rob Hardies, "Starr King President's Lecture" (speech, St. Louis, MO, June 24, 2006), Unitarian Universalist Association, uua.org/ga/past/2006/13158 .shtml. Rev. Rob Hardies summarized Rebecca Parker's theology using these words.

Yolanda Pierce's analysis of the popular movie *Black Panther* (2018) includes an insightful articulation of several themes inherent in African cosmology and religious practices. The movie draws from the cultural traditions of many real African concepts and her explanation identifies aspects of African cosmology depicted in the movie. Some of the examples of African cosmology she examines allow us to link African religious practices to the Black church and some of the norms common to Black Unitarian Universalists, including:

Ancestral veneration – In traditional Africa, the ancestors possess active roles and are honored even after their deaths. The veneration of the ancestors in African cosmology posits a thin veil between the living and the dead.

Spirit World – Diverse supernatural spirits and deities are capable of bestowing certain characteristics on human believers that defy logical explanation.

Traditional medicine – Medicine, applying the properties of plants and herbs to the healing and care of the human body, is sacred work. Knowledge of medicine is passed down through generations, usually by elders.

Priesthood/Clergy – The shaman, priest, conjurer, or healer also has the role of truth teller, wisdom keeper, and griot. People in this role act as mediators; their prophetic voices carry the messages of deities to the people.

Harmony and Balance – All of life is balanced, and this delicate balance is required for everything to function justly and peacefully.[5]

---

5   Yolanda Pierce, "African Cosmologies: Spiritual Reflection on the Black Panther Movie," Religion News Service, February 19, 2018, religionnews.com/2018/02/19/african-cosmologies-spiritual-reflections-on-the-black-panther-movie.

the stench of slavery in their souls. These women were energized, empowered, and inspired by teachings that were called Christian but were also deeply connected to African spiritual heritages. Many maroon communities in the Americas, groups of formerly enslaved, self-liberated Africans and their descendants, were headed by women for whom knowledge of mystical African metaphysics was a key to survival.[6] African American women such as Harriet Tubman, Sojourner Truth, and Ida B. Wells were rooted in West African cultural conceptions of spiritual power, economic prowess, physical strength, and political authority as shared by all genders.[7] Some women of African descent in the colonies possessed spiritual abilities that allowed them to communicate with ancestor spirits and create healing rituals, predict events, and translate dreams and visions. Many feared these women and many assumed they were charlatans. Some recognized their gifts. Some of these women were Christian evangelists.

Elizabeth (1766-1867), known by her first name only, was born to enslaved parents who belonged to the Methodist Society. She led her first prayer meeting in Baltimore in 1808 and was the earliest Black female preacher in recorded history. She recalled how, at the age of five, "she often felt the overwhelming presence of the Lord's Spirit, without at all understanding what it meant." She explained, "These incomes and influences continued to attend me until I was eleven years old."

> I saw with my spiritual eye, an awful gulf of misery. As I thought I
> was about to plunge into it, I heard a voice saying, "rise up and pray,"
> which strengthened me. I fell on my knees and prayed the best I could

---

6 Nubia Kai, interview with the author, December 24, 2020.
7 Dianca London Potts, "Holy Spirits: The Power and Legacy of America's Female Spiritualists," *Shondaland*, October 10, 2018, shondaland.com/live/a23652668/legacy -of-spiritualists.

the Lord's Prayer.... Immediately there appeared a director, clothed in white raiment. I thought he took me by the hand and said, "come with me." He led me down a long journey to a fiery gulf, and left me... I heard a voice say, "weep not, some will laugh at thee, some will scoff at thee, and the dogs will bark at thee, but while thou doest my will, I will be with thee to the ends of the earth.[8]

Elizabeth met with individuals in her first prayer meeting in Baltimore in 1808. She preached for about fifty years and retired to Philadelphia, where she lived among the Quakers.[9]

Jarena Lee (1783-?) became the first Black woman to preach at the African Methodist Episcopal (AME) Church founded by Bishop Richard Allen. The Bethel AME Church was founded in 1794 in Philadelphia, Pennsylvania, after Black members were pulled from their knees while praying by white officials at St. George's Methodist Episcopal Church. After Allen heard Lee preach, she reported,

I now sat down, scarcely knowing what I had done, being frightened. I imagined that for this indecorum, as I feared it might be called, I should be expelled from the church. But instead of this, the Bishop rose up in the assembly, and related that I had called upon him eight years before, asking to be permitted to preach, and that he had put me off; but that now he as much believed that I was called to that work, as any of the preachers present.[10]

---

8 Riggs, *Can I Get a Witness?*, 3-5.

9 Kenyatta R. Gilbert, "Hidden Figures: How Black Women Preachers Spoke Truth to Power," *Scalawag*, February 9, 2019, scalawagmagazine.org/2019/02/hidden-figures -how-black-women-preachers-spoke-truth-to-power.

10 "Jarena Lee," History of American Women, womenhistoryblog.com/2012/02/jarena -lee.html.

Zilpha Elaw (c. 1790-1873) experienced visions of divine inspiration and terrifying images accompanied by copious weeping for days on end before she received her call to preaching. She stated,

> I became such a prodigy to this people, that I was watched wherever I went; and if I went out to tea with any of the friends, the people would flock around the house where I was; and as soon as they judged the repast was finished, they came in and filled the house, and required me to minister to them the word of life, whether I had previously intended to preach or not. The people became increasingly earnest in their inquiries after truth; and great was the number of those who were translated out of the empire of darkness into the Kingdom....[11]

Rebecca Cox Jackson (1795-1871), a free Black woman born in Pennsylvania, began having visions as a child. As an adult, she became an influential Shaker and founder of her own Shaker community in Philadelphia. Jackson wrote about her visions and mediumship in her autobiography, titled *Gifts of Power*. She used her abilities to challenge racism and sexism and created spaces for Black women in her home. She held séance circles and communicated with the dead.[12]

Sojourner Truth (c. 1797-1883) escaped John Dumont's slave plantation in 1828. She made her way to New York City, where she became an itinerant preacher. She also became active in the abolition and suffrage movements. One of her legacies is her historic speech "Ain't I a Woman?" delivered at the Woman's Rights National Convention on May 29, 1851, in Akron, Ohio. Seven years later, white male hecklers

---

11 Riggs, *Can I Get a Witness?*, 13.
12 Potts, "Holy Spirits."

questioned her gender while she was addressing a congregation in northern Indiana. They asserted she was male because they thought her voice sounded masculine. The white men demanded that she show her breasts to prove her gender. In an era when it was considered immodest for women to show their ankles, Sojourner Truth demonstrated no shame in her body and exposed her breasts, thus shaming the men who attempted to humiliate her.

Harriet Jacobs (1813 or 1815 to 1897) hid in a crawl space in an attic for seven years to escape slavery. She was able to channel the voices of others and successfully opened a Spiritualist Sunday School in Boston. In 1861, she wrote her famous memoir *Incidents in the Life of a Slave Girl.*

Julia A. J. Foote (1823-1901) was the first woman ordained as a deacon in the African Methodist Episcopal Zion Church in 1884. In 1890, she was ordained as an elder.

Harriet E. Wilson (1825-1900), author, abolitionist, and trance speaker, was publicized in 1867 in the *Banner of Light*, a Boston-based spiritualist newspaper. She became one of the first Black women to publish a novel in 1859, titled *Our Nig: Sketches from the Life of a Free Black.*

It is this first wave of prophetic Black female preachers on whose shoulders Black Unitarian Universalist clergy women stand. It represents a lineage of Black female preachers intuitively guided by an African cosmology that was written in their very souls. These women carried the word at a time when it was not convenient or safe due to their gender and race. Virginia E. Walker Broughton, a Baptist missionary who served in Tennessee from 1887 until her death in 1934, describes some of the dangers:

In some places church houses were locked against our Bible women, and violent hands even laid upon some. Dear Sister Nancy C. said had not Sister Susan S. come to her rescue she would have been badly beaten for attempting to hold a woman's meeting in her own church.[13]

THE LEADERSHIP OF WOMEN IN EARLY CHRISTIANITY

Even the most cursory examination of early Christianity, first century AD, confirms the presence and leadership of women. Here are some examples[14]:

Acts 21:9—The four daughters of Philip the Evangelist are identified as prophetesses.

Acts 18: 25-26—Priscilla, or Prisca, and her husband Aquila are cited as fellow laborers in Christ.

Acts 16:40—Lydia, an associate of Apostle Paul, is described as a Christian leader who opened her home for ministry. She and other women are depicted as functioning in a pastoral capacity.

Confessions of St. Augustine, Bishop of Hippo—St. Monica, an Ethiopian and mother of St. Augustine of Hippo, is revered today in the Catholic and Orthodox Churches for her Christian virtues, her prayerful life, and her pious acts. Through her patience and tenacity, she eventually converted Augustine to Christianity. Upon her death, her dying words were, "Please remember me at the altar of God."

13 Riggs, *Can I Get a Witness?*
14 Richard M. Riss, "A Brief History of Some Women in Ministry," God's Word to Women, godswordtowomen.org/richardriss.htm.

Some of the women's calls to ministry were preceded by compelling and dramatic visions commanding them to commit their lives to preach and share the word of God. Others were simply motivated by the compelling and passionate belief that God had called them to preach the gospel. While these early preaching women met with resistance, they found ways to follow their sacred callings.

These brave women and others like them whose names we do not know paved the way and opened doors for other mid- to late nineteenth-century Black female preachers who fought for the right to preach the gospel. They lived segregated by race and separated by sex and drew on their culturally grounded theologies and own life experience, which they infused into Christianity, giving it meaningful new interpretations.

Origins of the Black Church

Unitarian Fannie Barrier Williams, a social reformer affiliated with All Souls Church in Chicago, eloquently characterized the way that the Bible was initially weaponized against enslaved people:

> Religion, like every other force in America, was first used as an instrument and servant of slavery. All attempts to Christianize the negro were limited by the important fact that he was property of a valuable and peculiar sort, and that the property value must not be disturbed, even if his soul were lost. If Christianity could make the negro docile, domestic and less and less independent and fighting savage, let it be preached to that extent and no further. Do not open the Bible too wide.[15]

---

15 Fannie Barrier Williams, "Religious Duty to the Negro" (speech, World's Parliament of Religions, Chicago, IL, September 22, 1893), Speaking While Female Speech Bank, speakingwhilefemale.co/religion-williams.

The Christianity that slave owners attempted to foist upon enslaved peoples to domesticate them was not the Christianity that birthed freedom fighters like Harriet Tubman and Sojourner Truth. It was not the same Christianity that female evangelists and preachers embraced. Their adaptability, innovation, and resilience transformed Christianity and birthed a liberatory religion that impassioned and inspired the first wave of prophetic Black female preachers.

The Black Church, since its inception, has embraced a strong social justice orientation as a result of the forced enslavement and racial injustices against its founding members. Black enslaved people found a deep and abiding message in the Christian stories of Jesus' suffering and his triumphant resurrection because the stories related to their own lived experiences. Thus they decolonized the Christian religion to represent for them hope, resistance, and deliverance in their time of adversity. Authors C. Eric Lincoln and Lawrence H. Mamiya contend that the Black church has been one of the few stable and coherent institutions to emerge from slavery. Furthermore, they confirm that the Black Church was in fact a focal point for Black people before and after slavery:

> After the Civil War the Black church was the main mediating and socializing vehicle for millions of former slaves, teaching them economic rationality, urging them to get an education, helping them keep their families together, and providing the leadership for early Black communities.[16]

An equally significant role of the Black Church was as an agent of resistance and change. Numerous slave insurrections took place in the South. Black preachers played a major role in resisting the institution of slavery. The planned insurrections of spiritual leaders Gabriel Prosser

---

16 C. Eric Lincoln and Lawrence H. Mamiya, *The Black Church in the African American Experience* (Durham: Duke University Press, 1990), 15.

(1800) and Denmark Vesey (1822) and the rebellion of Nat Turner (1831) depict the strong connection between liberation, religious calling, and activism that surfaced in the evolving liberation theology of the day. These events represented reverberations of a slave religion that had transformed itself into an emancipatory theology. These Black religious insurrectionists embraced the belief that oppressed peoples are called to God to carry out special tasks of liberation; hence, the significance of Black preachers' involvement in slave revolts. Slave owners' efforts to use Christianity to foster "obedient and docile" slaves were thwarted.[17] Instead, more than 250 slave revolts have been documented in the United States. These slave revolts included runaways, plantation revolts, ship mutinies, maroon guerilla warfare, and alliances with Indigenous people such as Mexicans and Native Americans.

Between 1890 and 1906, repression of both freed Black people and the Black Church intensified. From 1890 to 1920, a wave of legislation passed throughout the South disenfranchising Black people and permitting legal lynching and other forms of racial terror.[18]

If individual "renegade preachers" were a threat to the institution of slavery, then abolitionist clergy and their congregations posed an even greater one. One noteworthy example was Bishop Richard Allen and members of his congregation, who risked their freedom and lives to aid escaped slaves. The African Methodist Episcopal Zion Church became known as the "freedom church" because it was the spiritual home to many key abolitionists, such as Frederick Douglass, Harriet Tubman, and Sojourner Truth.

In addition, outspoken female abolitionists such as Frances Ellen Watkins Harper, a Unitarian, and Ida B. Wells courageously spoke out against the "peculiar institution."

---

17 Lincoln and Mamiya, *The Black Church*, 15.
18 Lincoln and Mamiya, *The Black Church*, 28.

Marginalization of Women in the Black Church and the Civil Rights Movement

Many scholars cite the civil rights era as one of the most definitive and significant periods in the history of Black people. The major accomplishments of the civil rights movement include:

- calling sustained national and international attention to the plight of Black people, claiming moral authority, and achieving legal authority
- the mobilization and creation of Black revolutionaries and conscious social movements
- the successful use of boycotts as a strategy to dismantle Jim Crow laws

Women in general, but particularly Black women, were rendered nearly invisible in the civil rights movement although they were functioning in leadership roles. The media played a role in this marginalization, focusing the nation's attention on the male leaders. The all-male line up of respected religious leaders included Rev. Martin Luther King Jr., Rev. Ralph David Abernathy, Rev. Fred Shuttlesworth, Rev. Jesse Jackson, and Rev. Andrew Young. As a result, many still perceive the movement as led by men and have little to no awareness of the leadership of Ella Baker, Fannie Lou Hamer, and Jo Ann Robinson. And although Rosa Parks galvanized the entire nation by refusing to give up her seat and catalyzing the Montgomery Bus Boycott, few know about her six decades of activism or know the name of Mary Fair Burks, who played a leading role in initiating the boycott after Parks was arrested.

This is hardly surprising for a movement rooted in the Black Church, which has resisted giving women the power of the pulpit. Scholar Evelyn Lorine Ogletree observes,

Within the church, the African American woman has played an active role in the advancement of this institution. Though frequently deemed the backbone of the family and the church, the African American woman has encountered trials within the church, which have limited the number of available opportunities. Lack of opportunities in church leadership is directly attributable to the female status. Specifically, African American women who are pastors experience gender inequity of leadership positions in the Black church, thus affecting salary and responsibilities.[19]

In spite of gradual improvements in recent years, discrimination based on gender is still present en masse across Black Protestant denominations in the United States. These instances of oppression have decreased opportunities for Black women to participate in their church communities as pastors.

And yet the ministries of Black women offer something unique and precious to the world. Marcia Y. Riggs, in her theological context, defines the features of prophetic religious tradition of Black women as follows:

> the recognition of an interrelationship between oppression for Blacks in American society and other people of color; an awareness of a connection between the oppression of Blacks and women in terms of misuse of power to subvert justice; and an acknowledgment of distinctive aspects of oppression for Black women; a sense of racial obligation and duty; and belief in both the justice of God and justice for Blacks as a command of God.[20]

19 Evelyn Lorine Ogletree, "Voices of Four African American Women Clergy and Their Perceptions of Gender, Equity and Leadership Styles" (PhD diss., 2012, Texas A&M University), oaktrust.library.tamu.edu/bitstream/handle/1969.1/148281/OGLETREE-DISSERTATION-2012.pdf.
20 Marcia Y. Riggs, "The Socio-Religious Ethical Tradition of Black Women: Implications for the Black Church's Role in Black Liberation," *Union Seminary Quarterly Review* 43 (1989), 119-132.

Black Unitarian Universalists:
What Beckons Us and What Drives Us Away

Rev. Michelle Bentley, the second Black woman called as a senior minister by a UU congregation, recalls her observations after talking with other Black UU ministers in the late 1980s:

> Theologically we were all on the same wavelength. I experienced intellectual camaraderie, a common thread of activism, and strong social justice backgrounds. We were all around the same age, young, Black, and gifted. Many of them were from middle class backgrounds and represented what Dubois referred to as the "talented tenth." All were down to earth and conveyed a sense of hospitality. We were all spiritual seekers. Each of us felt some pain and suffering for people and the world and we wanted to address it.[21]

In the early nineties, Rev. Marjorie Bowens-Wheatley, a Black UU clergy woman who served as adult programs director for the Religious Education Department of the Unitarian Universalist Association from 2000 to 2003, interviewed twenty-eight Black members of five congregations started by Black UU ministers. The survey identified the common profile of the Black members as "people in historically Black churches who are unhappy with a dogmatic theology and authoritarian structures." These same individuals, contended Bowens-Wheatley, were attracted to Unitarian Universalism because they were "in search of a place where spiritual or theological diversity is encouraged." Furthermore, she identified two conditions that contributed to the successful recruitment of new Black members to UU congregations:

---

21 Michelle Bentley, "Ain't I a Woman," in *Leaping From Our Spheres: The Impact of Women on Unitarian Universalist Ministry,* ed. Gretchen Woods (Boston: UUMA Center Committee, 1998), 35.

- tolerance for theist perspectives and an honoring of Jesus as a source of great inspiration for the African American community

- an educational process on issues of polity that values the positive contributions of the Black Church.[22]

Bowens-Wheatley noted the difficulties in building multicultural congregations and asserted that training was clearly indicated for clergy, lay leaders, and new start covenant congregations. Her training recommendations emphasized:

- valuing and honoring differences in worship and leadership styles based on racial, cultural, and class context

- comparative polity, including the pros and cons of how UU congregations were governed

Black Lives of Unitarian Universalism (BLUU) carried out a survey in the fall of 2017 with Black Unitarian Universalists and got feedback from 137 respondents. The majority of survey participants began attending Unitarian Universalist congregations in the previous five years. They were geographically dispersed with about 33 percent residing in the South and about 32 percent residing in the central east region of the United States. Thirty-three of the respondents were ages forty-five to fifty-four and another thirty-three between the ages of fifty-five and sixty-four. When asked what felt healing in the Unitarian Universalist context, 114 said "small group settings" and 97 chose "talking with someone one-on-one."

Most of the respondents indicate that they felt a deep sense of isolation and relied heavily on social media, particularly the BLUU closed

---

22 Marjorie Bowens-Wheatley, New Start Congregations: An Assessment.

Facebook group, to connect with other Black Unitarian Universalists. Responses indicate that Black Unitarian Universalists overwhelmingly tend to become a part of UU congregations because of the theology, not because of the community, and often find tensions between the established white-dominant culture and the more communal experience Black people tend to prefer. This cultural divide acts as an "exclusionary force in church life," according to BLUU. As a result, many Black people feel unwelcome in UU congregations. Some of the challenges identified by Black Unitarian Universalists in connecting with each other include lack of time, lack of money, location, and social anxiety. When asked about joy in their lives, "only a handful of those who are finding and maintaining joy in their lives mentioned church or a faith community as the reason. And of that handful, nearly half were referring to a community that was not UU." Black Unitarian Universalists appear to appreciate the Black-only spaces that BLUU has prepared. The overwhelming majority of respondents believed that organizing from a faith perspective with other Black Unitarian Universalists would be beneficial to them and their UU communities. Some of the common barriers cited to congregational membership include lack of diversity, lack of BIPOC people in leadership, uninspired preaching, failure to include racial justice work in social justice, lack of relationship building with local Black communities of direct action and negative attitudes about Black people among congregants.

Since there is so little published research on Black UU clergy women specifically, we must rely on anecdotal information for insight on what has particularly attracted Black women to Unitarian Universalism. I have initiated opportunities for Black UU women, both lay and clergy, to share their reflections in an online survey.

About twenty respondents replied to this question: What attracts Black women to Unitarian Universalism? Responses included "social justice," "inclusivity," "noncreedal," "religious education," and "friendliness."

Several respondents identified an appreciation of UU theology and also noted the diversity of UU theologies and the embrace and acceptance of that diversity. One respondent noted our "open and broad sources for faith and the broad embrace of different spiritual understandings." This was a common theme. Some respondents simply noted theology and others expressed very specific theologies that they were bringing with them. An atheist stated that she was "looking for a more diverse, intellectually rich environment."

Religious freedom is another strong theme that emerged. One respondent cited "the freedom to question, and even reject, mainstream faith—especially Christianity. To seek community without dogma." A respondent who identified as a religious humanist stated that her attraction was to the UU "search for meaning, social justice values, and religious community." Another mentioned "the idea that I could search for my own truth."

Other responses to my survey mentioned our welcoming of LGBTQ individuals and the desire for community with "spiritual and queer people of color," "promotion and nurturing of free thought & (promised) commitment to social justice," "The Sources and Principles of our faith," "promise of beloved community," "fellowship with similar values," and "Principle of inherent worth and dignity." One respondent's attraction to Unitarian Universalism was so uniquely individual and touching: "the idea that music is evidence of God."

Anti-Christian bias within Unitarian Universalist communities can drive away Blacks raised in theistic traditions, even when they are attracted to our religious freedom. In fact, it can seem like our religious "freedom" doesn't apply to those who identify as Christian. This was the case with Maxwell Pearl, a transgender man who was a seminarian before his transition. Maxwell eventually left Unitarian Universalism to pursue ministry in the United Church of Christ tradition. He talked about his spiritual journey and the decision to leave:

I became a Unitarian Universalist about five years ago and until recently was a first-year seminarian at Pacific School of Religion in Berkeley, California. I grew up Presbyterian and then spent four years in a fundamentalist Christian denomination during my teenage/young adult years. I swore off organized religion for many years and started a Buddhist meditation practice about fifteen years ago, which I continue today.... One of my interesting processes lately is integrating my Buddhist practice with my reemerging exploration of Christian theology. I benefitted from my conversations with a local Unitarian Universalist minister of color, but I was pretty disturbed upon hearing about the history of racism that some UU ministers of color had experienced. I was originally drawn to Unitarian Universalism because it felt like a very non-threatening way to begin to be a part of a community of faith that embraced all of the aspects of my varied spiritual path and honored my progressive views as an important part of my spirituality.

I am no longer a UU and have become a member of the United Church of Christ. I have discontinued my goal to pursue UUA credentialing, and I am instead starting on the path toward credentialing in the UCC. I attribute my departure to a combination of factors. My heart leads me to identify strongly as a Christian, and within UUism, that is something that is often a challenge. I didn't want to have to worry about that, as well as dealing with issues of race and class, which themselves loom large for me personally. I have incredible respect for the way in which many faith traditions are embraced and honored by Unitarian Universalism. I am happy and thankful that UUism exists, but it's not my path. I identify basically as a Christian. I am mightily struggling with some of the core aspects of the Christian faith (such as the divinity of Jesus). I do fundamentally believe that there are many, many paths to the Divine, and mine is just one path.[23]

---

23 written correspondence between Maxwell Pearl and author, summer 2005.

Perhaps Christian social ethicist and theologian Emilie Townes spoke for many Black Americans when she said, "I am looking for a theology soaked in Blackness with liberation at the center."

Career Challenges

From the very beginning of our Unitarian, Universalist, and Unitarian Universalist traditions, non-white people who expressed an interest in ministry came up against barriers that impacted their formation and settlement, and in some cases completely derailed them. In his seminal work *Black Pioneers in a White Denomination,* UU historian Mark Morrison-Reed details the travails of Rev. Egbert Ethelred Brown and Rev. Lewis McGee's efforts to become fully integrated and accepted as ministers. The lack of parity with white ministers in the search for parish settlements has been a major obstacle for ministers of color. It has often been difficult for BIPOC women ministers to observe white women and white LGBTQ individuals make progress while they continue to struggle to be called. In some instances, settlements were unsuccessful because of cultural differences, assumptions about theology, pulpit styles, and cultural expression.

The obstacles for Black UU women clergy begin even before ordination. The cost of theological education is one of the first barriers to entry for Black UU women who aspire to ministry. This is improving as the two seminaries, along with the Unitarian Universalist Association, offer needed scholarships and assistance to reduce student debt.

Once enrolled, Black seminarians often struggle with internship supervisors who are not prepared to mentor and train non-white seminarians in ways and practices that are not Eurocentric and that embrace diversity and inclusivity.

Rev. Kimberly Quinn Johnson, a seminarian at the time of her statement, noted how important it was to her that she chose Rev. Rosemary Bray McNatt, a Black UU clergy woman, as her teaching pastor:

I made it clear that she was probably the primary person that I wanted, because one of my concerns is, What is it like to be an African American minister in this denomination when there aren't very many African American women ministers and there aren't that many African American women members? I really wanted to work with somebody who knows.

"I never got a chance to mentor an African American woman," said McNatt, "so I was really excited. I was like, "Yes! Finally!"[24]

Creating communities that feel welcoming to seminarians of color has become a mission and goal for both UU seminaries, Starr King School for the Ministry and Meadville Lombard Theological School, and both have made great progress. As the consciousness and awareness of leadership, boards, and faculty have expanded, so has the seminary culture. In addition, courses like Womanist theology, pastoral counseling in diverse settings, and postcolonial feminist theory, as well as courses on racism and sexism, are included along with the traditional UU courses such as UU polity and history. And both seminaries now have persons of color at their helm, Rev. Rosemary Bray McNatt at Starr King and Dr. Elías Ortega at Meadville Lombard.

After seminary, Black women on the path to UU ministry face a whole new uphill battle, finding employment. It's a tough job market for Black women UU ministers. It's telling that not one congregation with 550 members or more called a Black woman as senior minister until Rev. Jacqueline Brett was called as lead minister to the Eno River Unitarian Universalist Fellowship in Durham, North Carolina, a congregation with more than 700 members, in 2022. Hiring patterns start at the top. A controversy in 2017 highlighted the fact that all five regional leads who supervised the Unitarian Universalist Association

24 TK Barger, "Seminary 3.0," *UU World*, January 28, 2014, 28-32.

Congregational Life staff, and their supervisor, were white ministers. Since then, the administration of President Susan Frederick-Gray has worked to address the issue, but these efforts alone cannot alter the complexion of UU clergy in general. It is not about getting a few faces of color into the high-level meetings or on the chancel but creating the kind of diversity reflected in the larger society.

Two publications in the last few years have documented and raised awareness of micro and macro aggressions that disempower and undermine religious professionals of color in Unitarian Universalism, often threatening their careers: *Centering: Navigating Race, Authenticity, and Power in Ministry*, a 2017 book from the Committee for Antiracism, Anti-oppression, and Multiculturalism of the UU Ministers Association, and *Widening the Circle of Concern*, the report of the UUA Commission on Institutional Change, which was commissioned in response to the 2017 controversy.

Moving among and being in predominantly white spaces where Black UU clergy women are sometimes treated as guests, even those who have grown up in the faith, wears on the soul. Unitarian Universalism still favors white male ministers, and laity often view Black women clergy as less capable than others.[25] It is profoundly uncomfortable to feel like a stranger in one's own faith community with one's chosen people. While race is a social construct and not real, Unitarian Universalism will not be successful in dismantling racism and white supremacy culture in our movement if we don't talk about race and the meanings attached to it. Rev. Adam Lawrence Dyer, consultant for the UU Justice

---

25 A little over ten years ago this author served as a trainer for Beyond Categorical Thinking, a workshop that prepares congregations to expand their thinking and hiring patterns to include ministers of color, LGBTQ+ people, disabled people, and women. The training included an anonymous survey that returned very candid information about the attendees' beliefs. Far more than we expected indicated that they believed ministers of color are not only less qualified but less competent than white ministers.

Ministry in California, notes in a report," Spiritual communities have a critical role to play in dismantling bias and bigotry. Yet race is the most uncomfortable subject for UU congregations to engage."[26]

White Unitarian Universalists experience discomfort around topics of race, class, and culture, BIPOC people in many UU congregations are being asked to function as "race workers," that is to answer every question about race and to be representative of diversity. As a result, BIPOC people do not feel safe, supported, or held by their UU communities, according to Rev. Dyer. In the role of race worker, BIPOC people often feel excluded, unwelcomed, and treated as live novelties.[27]

In her essay, Rev. Dr. Yvonne Seon, the first Black woman ordained and fellowshipped as a UU minister in 1981, notes that she was in search for eight years. Clearly, UU congregations were not ready to accept a Black woman in the role of minister. When a lobster becomes crowded in its shell and is unable to grow anymore, it travels out to sea, hoping for relative safety, where it will begin to shed its shell. It is a terribly dangerous process. The lobster has to risk its life, because once it becomes naked and vulnerable, its life is in peril. But that is the only way it can grow.[28] Instinctively, the lobster is called to respond to the compelling urge to grow. Like the lobster, we humans can only grow by taking the risk to live out our purpose and call. Likewise, Black women called to UU ministry must travel out to dangerous waters with a faithful resolve that we will get through whatever challenges we encounter.

We cannot and will not forget the sacrifices that our parents, aunties, and Ancestors have made for us to be where we are. For we are the hopes

---

26 Rev. Adam Dyer, "Equity Ministry in California: Report from the Field" (Equity Ministry Network, Spring 2016).

27 ibid.

28 Rev. Laurie J. Ferguson, "Jesus: Not a Victim for Our Sins," *in The Book of Women's Sermons: Hearing God in Each Other's Voices.*, ed. Rev. E. Lee Hancock (New York: Riverhead Books, 1999), 102.

and dreams of an enslaved people's vision of freedom. But our experience does not always look like or feel like freedom.

This faith is flawed and imperfect, just as many of us are flawed and imperfect. Yet we are called to this faith and we chose to answer, and believed that Unitarian Universalism, in turn, chose us. Unitarian Universalism needs its Black UU clergy women, and we need Unitarian Universalism. Our transformation is tied up in our mutual growth and transformation, and we are integrally linked.

On most days, I am proud to be a member of the small but growing group of Black UU clergy women. On some days, I want to retreat and weep in solitude as I learn about the depths of pain and suffering that some of my sisters have experienced. Some are so traumatized that they refuse to speak about these incidents even years later. But I know because they tell me they are not ready to talk about it. They are not ready to be in a room full of white Unitarian Universalists. Some have left this faith altogether.

There is an African proverb that says, "If you want to go fast, go it alone. If you want to go far, go together." Building our spiritual capacity for such a time as this will require diligence, discipline, and confronting some hard truths. It will require that we go together. We will not all get to Beloved Community together, but we will, I hope, learn new ways of being in integrity with ourselves as we build Beloved Community together. We must seize every opportunity to throw off our shackles and stretch our creativity.

What Seminarians Are Telling Us

REV. CONNIE SIMON

The story of Black women clergy in Unitarian Universalism is a relatively recent one, not quite forty years old. Many of those pioneers are still active in ministry and academia, their wisdom and guidance accessible to the current generation of Black women seminarians who experience them now as mentors, professors, and colleagues and seek to follow in their footsteps. While focused on the future and their own visions of ministry, these students are also mindful of the past and the stories of those Black women clergy who paved the road on which they now travel.

Who are these ministers-in-formation? As of spring 2018, there were fewer than ten seminarians who identified as Black women and Unitarian Universalist. The majority of them were enrolled at the two Unitarian Universalist seminaries, Starr King School for the Ministry and Meadville Lombard Theological School; one attended Phillips Theological Seminary in Tulsa, Oklahoma. Many are part-time students. None are "birthright" UUs—they come from a variety of faith traditions ranging from unchurched to Wicca to Presbyterianism to the Word of Faith Evangelical and Fire Baptized Holiness. They are diverse in age, with the youngest in her twenties and several in their fifties. Some have multiple college and graduate degrees and are pursuing ministry as a second or third career. Not all are called to parish ministry; some intend to pursue community ministry or activism upon graduation.

Despite their diversity, all reported the experience of being "the only one" at one time or another at their school, in their congregation, or in some other UU environment. And all reported that they were "used to it" and have accepted this as a consequence of being a Black Unitarian Universalist. On the prospect of enrolling at a school she describes as a "white, cis, hetero, able-bodied, Christian-dominated student body with a handful of people with marginalized identities" and what that might mean to her identity as a Black woman, one said, "It would be weird to be the only one [or] one of few again like elementary, middle, and high school." Assimilation at some level is necessary for survival in a society rooted in white supremacy culture. While white UUs would like to believe that their liberal religious beliefs make them somehow immune from its effects, the culture of white supremacy indeed infects our congregations, our seminaries, and our denomination.

At the same time, these women, like all who come to the ministry, seek to come as their authentic selves. They want to believe the words of the Rumi poem that has become one of our favorite UU hymns, "Come, Come, Whoever You Are." They want to believe they are welcome in seminary and in the ministry as they are and in their full Blackness. Yet, sadly, that is not always the case. To survive and to thrive in Unitarian Universalism, Black women seminarians must engage in a delicate dance, balancing the need to assimilate and "fit in," the desire to abolish white supremacy culture and transform our world, and the desperate yearning to be their authentic selves as religious professionals. This is the struggle of today's Black women seminarians. The women surveyed identified several common experiences that mark this struggle and shape their ministerial formation.

Institutional Challenges

Anti-oppression work and dismantling white supremacy culture are front and center in Unitarian Universalism today, especially in our seminaries. However, institutional structures are often slow to change.

And those institutions are filled with individuals who are at various stages of wokeness. Many claim to be doing "the work," but only some are actually doing it. When asked how comfortable they feel as Black women in their respective seminaries, each woman shared at least one story of discomfort and even downright pain. One said she "sometimes feel[s] there is a gap of understanding in faculty about issues regarding oppression and their immediate effect and correlation to teaching style, project expectations, theology, style, etc." A Meadville Lombard student, while genuinely appreciative of her school's commitment to "the work," said that faculty often directed their lesson plans and teaching focus to white students, neglecting the needs of their Black students. This was not an uncommon experience. Many expressed discomfort at listening to lectures and discussions about what "we" must do to dismantle white supremacy culture, knowing that, as Black people, they were not part of that "we." It is painful to sit in a room and have the experience of your people—*your* experience—be talked about. Some faculty offer students the opportunity to caucus during such discussions, but when there is only one Black student in the room, with whom are they supposed to caucus? This feeling can be even worse in online classes. One shared her experience of watching classmates post their honest, and sometimes painful, comments after reading *The Racial Contract* as a class assignment and the instructor's inability to recognize the depth of the tension. Only after several students shared their feelings did the instructor see the need to address the issue. No one believed that their school was deliberately hurtful or insensitive to Black students, but all believe there is room for improvement. Are our schools doing "the work" to make the seminary experience meaningful, welcoming, and inclusive for Black students? As one says, it's "like pulling teeth, avoiding it, dipping a toe in then celebrating, falling back asleep, getting checked, wandering in shame for a frustrating amount of time, denying and admitting, then tiptoeing towards it again." Yes, there is room for improvement.

Tokenism

None of the women questioned their call to the ministry, their fitness to serve, or their capacity to complete the academic requirements of seminary. However, some did question whether their acceptance was due, even in small part, to their identity as Black women. As one put it while rubbing her brown skin, "do they want me or do they really want *this*?" Another commented that, due to their small number at a time when the denomination is focusing so much on antiracism and anti-oppression, Black seminarians are almost a novelty, on display for all to see. Those who gawk are not always unkind; rather the experience is like being a "cute tiger cub in the zoo" that everyone wants to see and fawn over. They're a curiosity, a prize to be held up as an example of what is possible in UUism. Their pictures grace school marketing materials as evidence of the institution's diversity and they are asked to participate in various activities as representatives of marginalized communities. A student who identifies themself as a "Black trans person in a relationship with a woman" mused that their school had "hit the jackpot" in recruiting them and wondered if "people want me [for who I am] or because I check off boxes for them." Today's Black female seminarians are realists. They acknowledge and suffer the burden of tokenism and see it for what it is, evidence that their ministries are so badly needed in this faith.

Microaggressions, White Fragility, and Vulnerability

All the interviewed seminarians reported incurring microaggressions on a regular basis—not just in seminary, but in their congregations and in their lives. At General Assembly 2018 in Kansas City, there was a running joke among Black and brown religious professionals about how many times they had been called by someone else's name, as though they all looked alike or their identities were interchangeable.

Microaggressions happen every day as people make assumptions or question Black UU women's hair, personal appearance, politics, faith background, theology, etc. This is not new. However, those seeking to enter the ministry must use extra care in how they choose to respond. If they call out the microaggressor, they may encounter white fragility and be accused of being the stereotypical Angry Black Woman who hurt "Becky's" feelings when everyone knows Becky didn't mean any harm, has only the best of intentions, has a good heart, doesn't have a racist bone in her body, has been a UU for years, and, most importantly, has many Black friends.

For many Black seminarians, fear of being labeled the Angry Black Woman is real. It has the potential to end a ministerial career even before it starts. Having a reputation as an Angry Black Woman is perceived as threatening success at the Ministerial Fellowship Committee and in the search process. As a result, many confess to sometimes withdrawing from potentially harmful interactions and distancing themselves from certain relationships and situations for self-preservation. One recalled a particularly sensitive incident in which she wanted to be "just another person" attending a school event but, as the victim of a white person's microaggression and extreme fragility in response, suddenly feeling cheated and vulnerable. "I was having a good day, and she [the fragile white classmate] took that away from me." These strong, capable, vibrant Black women, who have so much to offer to Unitarian Universalism, feel compelled to withhold a portion of themselves from their seminary experience and their faith! How are these future ministers expected to lead their congregations in the fight for justice and the recognition of the inherent worth and dignity of all persons if they are required to suppress their own worth and dignity?

Community

Despite the discomfort, frustration, pain, and weariness they face on a regular basis, each woman shared the importance of community to their seminary experience. Very few found support in their local Unitarian Universalist Ministers Association (UUMA) chapter, and there were varying degrees of involvement and satisfaction with the UUMA's Ministerial Formation Network. While some were involved with or followed Black Lives of Unitarian Universalism (BLUU) and Diverse & Revolutionary Unitarian Universalist Multicultural Ministries (DRUUMM), they did not find these groups particularly helpful to them in their formation as seminarians. Rather, most cited Finding Our Way Home (FOWH), the annual gathering of UU religious professionals of color, as their most valuable source of connection, rejuvenation, and spiritual healing. As much as they enjoy FOWH, many expressed the need for more structured opportunities at the event for clergy/seminarian interaction.

While grateful for the contributions of those who came before them, today's Black women seminarians know the road ahead is not yet clear and smooth. One recalled seeing her previous minister, a Black woman, "run out of the church" after the congregation was "openly nasty" to her, causing this seminarian to be forever cautious about who she trusts. She, like many of the students interviewed, expects to be treated differently as a Black UU minister than her white colleagues. Nevertheless, to paraphrase Senator Mitch McConnell, she and her colleagues persist. Today's Black female seminarians are fierce, committed, and dedicated to this faith and to helping Unitarian Universalism live into its promise of Beloved Community.

MINISTERIAL JOURNEYS AND REFLECTIONS

The Sojourner Truth Congregation

REV. DR. YVONNE SEON
PRELIMINARY FELLOWSHIP 1981,
FULL FELLOWSHIP 1988

The Sojourner Truth Congregation of Unitarian Universalists was an experiment in diversity that grew from both the success and the failure of the Unitarian Universalist Association's antiracism campaign. The congregation started as a response of a number of people to the presence in the Unitarian Universalist ministry of the first African American woman, and their vision for her ministry—my ministry. That vision was driven by the disparity between the UUA goal of African American inclusion and my experience seeking settlement. The congregation's story cannot be separated from my personal journey toward ministry as it intersected the Association's encounter with the struggle for civil rights in America.

I grew up during the Great Depression and experienced the privation that went along with World War II. All my cousins spent time being cared for by my grandmother, and we went with her on Sundays to the charismatic Christian church three doors away. She lived in a Black neighborhood in Washington, DC. The church, a converted row house in the Shaw area, was filled on Sundays with the sounds of clapping, shouting, and jumping to the accompaniment of tambourines and a well-worn upright piano. Walking in the front door, one entered a large room with rows of chairs on either side of the aisle. At the front, an archway marked the edge of a raised area where the bishop, his deacons, and the choir sat—all dressed in various kinds of robes. On the arched wall, in large gilded letters, was printed, "God is Love."

This was my first lesson in theology, and it embraced all I needed to know. Nevertheless, I soon found that the chaotic sights and sounds of a church were a distraction from religious thought and behavior. As children, my cousins and I imitated the bishop's preaching style and laughed; we pretended to be various members of the congregation; we mocked their "amens" and "uh-hums," their faints and their swoons. But we got another view of religion and church at Grandma's house as she evolved in her own spirituality and ministry.

I witnessed my grandmother's religious evolution close up when I went to live with her while my mother was working in Baltimore as campaign manager for a candidate for the U.S. Congress. Mom risked her life running John Camphor's Progressive Party headquarters near the docks, knowing I was safe with her mother. Meanwhile, Grandma told of visions of impending world events. She fed the hungry. She shared resources with those in need, saving several small community businesses with a gift or loan at a critical juncture. She prayed for the sick.

In her spiritual life, my grandmother drew from religious traditions of the world. She burned incense in a seated figure of the Buddha. She fasted in sympathy with Mahatma Gandhi as he protested British rule over India. She designated an upper room as her "prayer garden," where she worshiped and laid hands on the sick and infirm. She placed a rack of votive candles and a prayer rug in front of the one window in the room, which faced east. She asked a talented artist of the church to paint a picture of Jesus in the Garden at Gethsemane on the north wall. (She insisted that Jesus be facing to the actual East in the painting.) A framed representation of Black Jesus and several hymnals were remnants from her time in New York, following Marcus Garvey. Everyone who entered her home was welcomed with "Salaam alaikum," the Islamic greeting of peace.

When my mother's baby sister reached high school age, she got permission to walk from Grandma's house to St. Luke's Episcopal Church.

I had been baptized there as an infant and begged her to take me along. I was six and able to read well enough to follow the liturgy in the *Book of Common Prayer*. I soon knew the creeds and many prayers by heart. I appreciated the simple chants and the quiet, structured worship of this Black congregation that practiced "high church."

When I was eight years old, my parents separated, and later divorced. In order to spend more time with my father, I started attending with him the Baptist church in which he grew up. One day, at age twelve, I found myself at the front of the church, asking to be baptized. My father, who was blind, went up with me and rejoined the church. We were both baptized a few weeks later. By the time I reached high school, Sunday morning church with Dad was an increasingly rare activity. But I was getting old enough to travel to church with my peers. I discovered that several friends were going to a small Episcopal church close enough for me to walk; I returned to the church tradition of my mother's side of the family.

In college, I began to question religion but never God. I questioned the concept of the trinity, the divinity of Jesus, and the ritual of Holy Communion. During my senior year at Allegheny College, I took a required course on religious traditions and Christian practices. The instructor was a Quaker who helped us explore the philosophy of non-violence and taught us to share in silence! We generally came out of silence trying to find justification for violence. Were there no exceptions to nonviolence?

During that semester, the subject of religion dominated conversations with my closest friends. As I expressed my views, someone said, "You sound like a Unitarian!" and suggested I visit the First Unitarian Church of Meadville, Pennsylvania. One Sunday, I went there alone in search of church community, a place where my personal beliefs were not out of place. That Sunday is one I will never forget. The minister spoke to my deepest beliefs about God and religion. I got up at the end of the service feeling full, wanting to share. But the members, all white, peeled off in every direction, speaking to one another. I was left standing alone in the middle of a pew near the center of the church. There were no hellos, no handshakes, and no words of welcome. It was as though I were invisible. Nevertheless, I walked back toward the entrance to greet the minister.

As I stood at the back of the line, I saw an African American woman coming up from the basement, carrying a tray of muffins for the coffee table. I moved out of line to greet her, but she quickly turned her back and returned downstairs without responding to my smile. Was there no church community there that could include African Americans? I wondered.

This initial encounter with Unitarian Universalism was in 1958, just as the civil rights movement was starting in earnest. Although I knew of All Souls Church, Unitarian, in my hometown of Washington, DC, I had never been there. All the churches I had attended to that point were filled with Black worshipers. I was aware, however, that All Souls Church was perhaps the only place in town where an interracial couple could worship together. I was also aware that the church had sponsored W.E.B. DuBois as a speaker the February after he had been shunned as a liberal and a Communist, and his reputation tarnished by the House Committee on Un-American Activities.

When my first Black and white friends at Allegheny heard about my experience at the First Unitarian Church of Meadville, they were confused. Neither the Unitarians nor the Universalists had ever excluded African Americans. I would later learn that Allegheny, the oldest liberal arts college west of the Allegheny Mountains, had in 1906 awarded a degree to one of the earliest African Americans to train for Unitarian ministry at the seminary in Meadville. Although he never pursued ministry, Don Speed Smith Goodloe went on to become the first principal of what became Bowie State University in Maryland.

My reintroduction to Unitarian Universalism would come much later. I had graduated from Allegheny College, traveled to Peru, and used a Woodrow Wilson Fellowship to complete an MA degree at the American University in Washington, DC. I had traveled to Kinshasa to work for the government of the country that would become Zaire, the Democratic Republic of the Congo. As executive director of the Inga Dam Project in the Congo, I had traveled to several other countries in Africa and in Europe. Everywhere I went, I searched for a spirituality that made sense to me. I would first try the prevailing Christian worship tradition. Sometimes this was Catholicism. Often, it was the regional Protestant church. In some of the cities, there was a Church of England, where I found the comfort of a familiar ritual in the language of my native land. So I continued to think of myself as Episcopalian and part of the church in which I had been baptized as an infant.

After returning home to Washington, DC, in May 1963, I ran into an old friend, who turned out to be a neighbor down the street. In October of 1966, we were married in a local Episcopal church, where we sang together in the choir. The following fall, we moved to Yellow Springs, Ohio, where I found work with Wilberforce University. Affiliated with the African Methodist Episcopal Church, Wilberforce was the first college in America founded by and for African Americans. There I began formal research on African and African American history and culture, including African traditional religions. I had stopped attending church but was discovering spiritual perspectives from African cultures that rang true for me.

Meanwhile, Wilberforce gave me two assignments that nudged me toward UU ministry. First, I was asked by the president of the university to serve as one of two representatives on the Consortium for Higher Education Religion Studies. In that capacity, I worked closely with the administration of Payne Theological Seminary, once part of Wilberforce. I was also invited to participate in a year-long symposium on African religions organized by Professor Newell Booth of Miami University of Ohio. Second, my primary assignment at the university was shifted to coordinator for Student Life Programs. In this latter capacity, I was visited by Professor Gene Reeves, chair of the philosophy department and a Unitarian Universalist minister.

It was my job to schedule speakers for the cultural development course, and Dr. Reeves suggested I consider inviting Rev. David Eaton, newly appointed senior minister of All Souls Church in Washington, DC. Dr. Reeves, one of several white instructors at this traditionally Black campus in southern Ohio, had had a role in linking Eaton, his classmate and friend at Boston University School of Theology, to the UUA. The well-respected Eaton was the first African American called to a major urban UU church. I agreed to invite him to Wilberforce.

Thus began a conversation with Gene Reeves about Unitarian Universalism, its stand on civil rights, its record in social justice, and more. When Rev. Eaton arrived, Dr. Reeves was his host. My family came to dinner. David Eaton spoke of his vision for Black participation in the UUA and invited my husband and me to come to All Souls whenever we returned to DC. For the first time, I saw Unitarian Universalism in a favorable light. When we returned to the DC area in 1973, I began attending with my children.

At All Souls, I felt community among Unitarian Universalists. I was excited about the excellent gospel choir, which was my entry point into participation. I attended my first General Assembly singing with the Jubilee Singers in Philadelphia. Soon thereafter, I was invited to participate in a seminar on the history and philosophy of the UU movement and to sign the membership roll. Having learned that King's Chapel in Boston had become the first Unitarian church in America when the minister removed all references to the trinity from the *Book of Common Prayer*, I was sure I was in the right place.

One Sunday, Rev. Eaton asked me to speak for a summer service, suggesting a topic related to my expertise in Africa as a possible subject matter. This was an important step on my path to UU ministry. I chose to speak on Mozambique's proximate achievement of African self-determination. Speaking that Sunday, it felt as though I belonged in the pulpit.

The actual call to ministry came in March 1979, as my grandmother lay dying in the group home where she had been cared for over many years. I rushed to be at her side. As I crossed the threshold to her room, I saw my grandmother open her eyes. She expired as she saw me walking to her bedside, giving me her last breath as a legacy. I took this as a sign that I was being called to continue her ministry of compassion and healing. Closing her eyes, I silently committed to the call.

Meanwhile, the minister who funeralized my grandmother introduced me to Rev. Dr. Leon Edward Wright. Dr. Wright was a New Testament scholar and mystic who helped me move forward with this "call," recognizing me as a "channel for the flow-through of the love of God." I also talked it over with my minister, Rev. Eaton. He asked me, "Do you want to be a minister?" I replied, "It's not something that one 'wants.' I don't have a choice; it's a calling." Rev. Eaton agreed to support my application to Howard University Divinity School. He warned, however, that I would be challenged both as Black and female within the UUA. Women were generally consigned to ministry as religious educators, and at that point, as far as we knew, there were no African American women trained in ministry or moving toward parish ministry. He also spoke of the suspicion many UUs would have of my nonrational spirituality. That fall, I entered Howard University's Divinity School as a single parent supporting three offspring. . . .

While in divinity school, I was invited to a spiritual retreat led by Dr. Wright. He talked about the healing ministry of Jesus, and we were encouraged to "follow" rather than to "imitate" Jesus. He taught us to meditate daily as part of the process of staying attuned to God's will for our lives. I was reminded to re-read Ralph Waldo Emerson's "Divinity School Address" and study the Transcendentalist movement....

Soon after I entered Howard University Divinity School, family and friends began to call on me to minister to them. They encouraged me to start a church. I asked at school for permission to use the old chapel on the main campus of Howard for a weekly Wednesday afternoon service. Generally, twelve to twenty people attended regularly. They began planning for fundraising, a regular meeting place, and an organizational structure. An attorney worked on incorporation papers for the Garden of Gethsemane. A dentist whose wife was a friend of my mother volunteered to serve as chair of the Board. We asked to use the chapel of the divinity school for a formal opening in the spring of my senior year. I graduated a few weeks later, in May 1981.

Because the UUA was being challenged to be intentional about diversity, my name was included as a candidate for several searches. I was kept busy preparing packets. But search committees generally wasted no time explaining why I was not a match.

In fall 1981, I was ordained by All Souls; a few weeks after, I presented myself to the Ministerial Fellowship Committee. The Committee gave me conditional approval. I worked with Rev. Eaton to satisfy the conditions to prepare for the event. On November 23, 1981, over two hundred clergy and laypersons gathered at All Souls Church to affirm and support my call to ministry. Two months later, Adele Smith-Penniman became the second Black woman minister to be ordained. I began to communicate with the UU Office of Ministry in Boston and to prepare a packet to use in the settlement process.

Because the UUA was being challenged to be intentional about diversity, my name was included as a candidate for several searches. I was kept busy preparing packets. But search committees generally wasted no time explaining why I was not a match. Meanwhile I continued to minister to the members of the Garden of Gethsemane. UU colleagues invited me to join the Greater Washington Area Religious UU Professionals. I received invitations to speak at UU congregations and fellowships in the region. Honoraria for these sermons ranged from $100 to $250 each. My income varied from $200 to $400 a month. My estranged husband was underemployed and not contributing to support the children except when they were with him in Ohio. With three to feed, clothe, and shelter in addition to myself, I had to find a settlement or another job very soon. I went to Rev. Eaton for help.

Rev. Eaton suggested that I apply for a grant from the All Souls Beckner Fund to support me in UU campus ministry at Howard University. The award was enough to support me for about six months. I attended weekly meetings with other chaplains and Dr. Evans Crawford, the dean of Chapel. When the Lenten season arrived, I realized that the planned program would exclude all who were not Christian. I proposed to Dean Crawford that each chaplain make a presentation regarding his faith tradition under the umbrella of "Seasons of Spiritual Renewal." The dean asked me to coordinate the program. As the chaplaincy neared an end, David Eaton called me in to suggest full-time work with the District of Columbia Public Schools. I applied and was hired. I continued to pastor the Garden of Gethsemane and to submit packets when asked by the Office of Ministry.

Soon after my ordination, Elois Hamilton, an African American UU, and Werner Mattersdorf, both members of Davies Memorial Church, began to pay close attention to my path within the UUA. Elois, then president of the Prince George's County Chapter of the Southern Christian Leadership Conference (SCLC), was known throughout the county as an effective change agent. Werner was active on the Board of the SCLC chapter and a member of the Board of Davies Church. As part of their vision for a more inclusive UUA both Elois and Werner had a vested interest in seeing me settled as a UU minister.

Werner began to visit area churches and district conferences when he knew I would be speaking at them. The first time Cedar Lane Church in Bethesda, Maryland, invited me as guest speaker in 1982, Werner came to hear me. After that, whenever he learned of settlement options that seemed a possible fit for me, he would tell me about them and encourage me to seek to get my name on the list. Still, no congregation was ready to invite my candidacy. Werner was convinced that race and gender were factors. He began to take action on my behalf without my knowing it. Soon thereafter, Werner brought his wife, Anna, to visit the Garden of Gethsemane, and they came regularly to be spiritually fed. He began getting information that he hoped might lead to the Garden of Gethsemane becoming a UU congregation so that I might be settled there. Two things had occurred by then to convince him that, where my ministry was concerned, the UUA was neither open to nor prepared to include the diversity that I represented.

First, Davies Memorial was looking for a minister. The Search Committee was having trouble agreeing on someone. While I was never told this directly, I later suspected that my name had come up and that the Committee was not willing to consider my candidacy. Werner apparently spoke to some of the other Board members about having me serve in an interim capacity to give the Search Committee more time to complete its work. He may have also wanted to give the congregation an opportunity to experience my ministry as a way of confronting their concerns. At any rate, I received a call from the chair of the Board outlining the terms of a proposed contract to start the following Sunday. My first day in the pulpit, the Search Committee chairperson unexpectedly came up to make an announcement. She announced that the Committee had agreed on the new minister to be recommended and gave her name. I was convinced that the Committee had rushed to make a selection before the congregation had an opportunity to find out whether their fears about an African American were warranted. That same day, I was asked to be present to a husband whose wife had just died. I helped rally the congregation around the family and worked with the husband on funeral arrangements. From that time until my contract ended, members treated me as their "real" minister. A bonding occurred, and we parted without malice.

The second wake-up call occurred when I asked to be considered for the UU United Nations Office. I knew that I was a strong candidate because of my background in political science and international affairs, and because of my fluency in French. I was invited to interview. During our conversation, the interviewers intimated that they were concerned that I would not remain for five years. I had not been aware that this was a criterion. Moreover, it was not clear that others would be asked for a five-year commitment. Sure enough, the Search Committee selected the other finalist—or finalists: a couple who would both work in the job for the price of one!

Werner saw this selection as unfair competition. He was incensed and wanted to sue the UUA. I was tired and still needed a job. I asked Werner not to sue so that instead I would have time to focus on finding a way to support my offspring. I had now been in the search process for nearly eight years. It was then that Werner suggested we launch a campaign to make my existing ministry at the Garden of Gethsemane an official settlement. I contacted David Eaton, who suggested we talk to Sid Peterman, our district representative. Sid came to DC to brainstorm strategies for getting me settled. He, Werner, and David agreed that it was time for the UUA to take some responsibility. It was the fall of 1987. Werner agreed to work with a committee of the Garden of Gethsemane to affiliate with the UUA. Peterman agreed to look for funding possibilities for a "new start" congregation. He also agreed to consult with Tom Chulak and Lucy Hitchcock, who were working with urban UU ministries.

By the General Assembly of 1989, the Southeast Congregation of Unitarian Universalists was voted into UUA affiliation. Some of the members had created a banner for the opening parade at GA. The group had a regular meeting place for Sunday morning worship. We had hired someone to help open the auditorium we used on Sundays. About twenty-eight members signed the roll. Initially, the membership was truly diverse, a mixture of Black and white, male and female, young people and seniors, gay and straight. We found space for a small office in the basement of a community center at Ninth Street and Pennsylvania Avenue, Southeast. Later, we rented a large room on the first floor so that office space and worship space were in the same place. The UUA organized meetings and retreat sessions during which we articulated our mission as "an intentionally diverse religious community," agreed on a covenant, developed an advertising campaign, and discussed ways to raise money and increase visibility. Around this time, the suggestion was made that we find a more suitable name. The name Sojourner Truth Congregation of Unitarian Universalists was put forward. Another member agreed to bring in information about Sojourner Truth's life so that the membership could make an informed decision. Members volunteered for various tasks related to the organizing, training, and performing of a drama group for youth. The proposed new name made it a natural to call them the Youth of Truth. The vote the following Sunday was unanimous in favor of the new name.

The congregation grew slowly but steadily. The UU church of Arlington, Virginia, committed to a buddy relationship. Several people came in specifically to work with the drama group. One worked on scheduling performances of the group's first play, an anti-drug drama called "Undercover Bird." Elois Hamilton organized pizza parties for the group and allowed them to meet in space rented by the Prince George's County SCLC. A professional actor and director of Black theater agreed to coach the group in dramatic technique. The congregation was so proud of the achievements of the youth that they agreed to send them to perform at General Assembly in Hartford, Connecticut. Funds were found to send four youth to GA: William and David Chappelle, Masavia Greer, and Rachel Walker. Their performance called attention to drug-related crime and youth homicide rates that had reached epidemic levels in DC. "Is it more important to save the whales or save Black males?" their presentation asked in a humorous sketch. A near-capacity audience received the group with resounding applause.

The following year, members of the congregation began to spend more time in disagreements over the means of achieving what should have been common goals. Church politics overshadowed the spiritual grounding of the group. Board meetings became gripe sessions, with one faction trying to score points over another and everyone thinking they knew better than the minister. In addition, UUA funding for the new start was being scaled back to encourage greater self-reliance. Some members were convinced that priorities would have shifted and that this was a time for downsizing rather than growth. Some questioned whether they could afford a minister. I wondered whether they could afford not to have a minister.

There came a point when it appeared that Black, straight members were in battle with white, gay members for control. When a Black jazz musician joined the congregation, the white pianist had trouble cooperating with him to share responsibility for the music and to create more diversity of musical styles. The Black jazz musician stopped coming to church. A white woman who lived in the neighborhood was attracted to the message of hope in my sermons. However, she wrote me explaining that she could not sign the book because of an unpleasant personal encounter with members outside of the worship service. A gay member of the church began to advertise the congregation in the *Blade* newspaper. He did this without the knowledge or consent of either the minister or the board of directors. The ads seemed to promise services or special outreach that were too much for the young congregation to deliver. . . . I began to feel burned out as I tried to negotiate these conflicts while maintaining my own spiritual center and nurturing the spirituality of the congregation.

In the end, the money for the new start ran out. But before that happened, the members of the congregation who had the initial vision began to slip away, one by one. Some moved to begin new lives in new places. Some became too ill to continue the struggle. Some, like me, were burning out. Those who were left were too much alike to spark creative tension. However, the vision that created Sojourner Truth Congregation of Unitarian Universalists had been made manifest within the UU movement. Another step had been taken and the denomination would never again be the same.

Black Resilience

REV. DR. ADELE SMITH-PENNIMAN
PRELIMINARY FELLOWSHIP 1982,
FULL FELLOWSHIP 1986

The cross burned outside the church where we held an organizing meeting, faded whitewashed clapboards facing a dirt road. Inside we sang all the more fervently. Freedom songs only strengthened the resolve of local citizens to register to vote come morning. *This little light of mine ... We shall not be moved ...* Summer 1965. Kershaw County, South Carolina.

We Northern students were trained by the greats of the Southern Christian Leadership Conference: Rev. Dr. King, Bayard Rustin, and Rev. Hosea Williams, as well as the ordinary citizens, the true heroes who risked job, home, and body for human rights and dignity. Our take-aways were far greater than what we gave. For me, one of the most compelling lessons was that religion can be a force for radical change. Without the church, it is doubtful the Civil Rights Act and the Voting Rights Act would have passed. De jure segregation would have persisted for another decade, if not longer.

A commitment to peace and justice brought me to religion, and its thread weaves through my ministry. Back in ninth grade, I was drawn to the deep corporate silence of Quaker (Society of Friends) worship. I found equally powerful their peace testimony and would often join their vigils on the Boston Common protesting U.S. military engagement in what was then called the Indochina conflict, this at a time when most Americans could not locate Vietnam on a map.

I remained an active Quaker until I graduated from college. (I returned to the faith after retirement and am currently a member of both a Friends Meeting and a UU congregation.) When I settled in New York City in 1968, I encountered a racist incident among Quakers that propelled me a few blocks west to the Riverside Church, a large interdenominational, interracial body with incredible music and a deep social justice commitment. It was there that a female minister became my mentor and I began taking steps toward seminary. I had been in a Ph.D. program in psychology at Columbia University and felt pastoral counseling might actually be a better fit, that perhaps it would foster less hubris and more closely match the questions people often carry into a clinical setting: Who am I? What gives value to my life? How do I live in right relationship?

I entered seminary under the auspices of the United Church of Christ, also my parents' faith. Harvard Divinity School was electric! A Muslim would be seated next to a Reform Jew next to a Missionary Baptist in a class led by a United Church of Christ (UCC) professor. Never before nor since have I witnessed such invigorating discussions. Furthermore, women were just beginning to enter seminary in numbers and we were rethinking Scripture, theology, history, and spirituality. People of color defined liberation theology and together—women, queer people, workers, and people of color—reclaimed the voices of so many who had been silenced. My studies and activism fed one another. I was also fortunate to represent the UCC on the National Council of Churches Commission on Women in Ministry and to be president of a student-led organization, Black Women in Ministry.

But before long, I had my personal version of the Trinitarian Controversy of the seventeenth and eighteenth centuries: how do I meld an all-encompassing sense of Mystery with a doctrine that speaks of Father [sic], Son [sic], and Holy Spirit? If I lived in an urban area, I could have found UCC parishioners with theological understandings similar to mine, but in seminary, I had married and settled in small town Massachusetts, where churches were more conservative. I graduated from Harvard without a denominational affiliation.

One of my lasting regrets is that I never sought dual UCC-UUA ordination. In the UCC, I found a vibrant African American presence that supported and challenged me during my seminary years and beyond. Painfully, I too often experience in Unitarian Universalism a dearth of siblings walking beside me or leading the way. Moreover, I suspect that to many Euro-Americans in UU leadership, I am invisible, an afterthought, or a token to prove they are "progressive." I struggle as well with the view prevalent in UU circles that being theologically "progressive" means excluding the rich language, music, rituals, and Scriptures foundational to many of the people with whom I seek dialogue. Congregants have chastised me for speaking of worship, prayer, and God. I yearn for a large universal table where many are welcomed—and the meal is all the richer for the distinct dishes we each bring. On a Sunday, you may find me at the local AME church or walking in the woods surrounding my home. I appreciate the liturgy of Christmas Eve and Easter services at Grace Episcopal. My daughter, initiated into the Jewish and Yoruba religions, further deepens my spirituality.

So what brought me to Unitarian Universalism, albeit reluctantly? And what has kept me? Except for fleeing into Arlington Street Church's sanctuary when Boston police on horseback charged peaceful demonstrators, I had never been in a UU church until sometime after seminary. Yes, I had met many Unitarian Universalists but my image of the Association was not positive—too white, too affluent, and overly intellectual. Fast forward and I was organizing with the Nuclear Freeze movement and my chapter met in the basement of a UU church. I was grateful that the congregation offered their space for free so I decided one Sunday to wander upstairs and look about. I was converted! I am drawn to a Unitarian Universalism that is noncreedal yet shaped by compelling Principles. Yes, my experience as a professional within the Unitarian

49

Universalist Association remains complex and sometimes troubled, but the Association is usually broad enough for my journey—whether in my agnostic, Theist, Buddhist, Afro-centric, or earth-based permutations.

Ordained in 1982, I closely followed Rev. Dr. Yvonne Seon, the first African American woman to receive fellowship. I then became the first to be settled and achieve final fellowship. I remember well my interview at a prominent multi-staffed church for my first position as a UU minister. I was asked how it might be for me to work in a predominantly white congregation. I began my reply sharing that I had spent much time in white settings, that on occasion there might be tensions, but that . . . (I was planning to stress staying in communication even when differences arise and believing most people are of good faith) . . . but the senior minister interrupted. "Adele, I beg to differ," he said, drawing up to his full six-foot-plus height. (I am barely taller than five feet.) "There will be no tensions. We are a *very* liberal congregation." I couldn't wait to flee; the mere acknowledgment that race and racism could be factors was taboo! I turned down the job offer and became co-director of the Women's Theological Center, an interfaith, multiracial womanist study/action/reflection program with a focus on empowering the people who are most marginalized.

In all my roles as an educator, clinician, preacher, and activist, I have brought a strong community focus to ministry. Faith-based social action, resting on a belief in the inherent worth of every person, is often less polarizing and more sustainable than a purely secular approach. And a parish at its best can be a significant conduit for change. In addition to directing justice organizations, I have served two Massachusetts congregations. It has been an honor to walk with people through life's transitions, the births and deaths, the joys and sorrows. I love being a minister!

However, in spite of forty years in ministry, I have no ready answers to how we African American women can bring our identities to our work without them being bruised and misunderstood, to paraphrase the late activist and writer Audre Lorde. The assaults are frequent, ranging from a fellow member of the Ministerial Fellowship Committee warning that we must not lower standards to diversify the pool of candidates to a Euro-American mother in my parish angrily denying that her adopted child was of African heritage. And too often UU structures—from oppressive "diversity" curricula to district executives who refused to look at how racism and classism crippled my ministry—maintain a status quo on the backs of people who don't mirror their archetype of the typical clergy. I have been traumatized by racist assaults made all the more destructive by the absence of UU leadership to help me navigate them. At times, I have needed to pull away, to regroup, to heal. Unfortunately, this means I have been less present to the African American clergy and laity who have come to the Association

At times, I have needed to pull away, to regroup, to heal.

more recently. I am still not strong enough to attend chapter meetings or General Assembly. But my hope is that one day I will be able to more fully reach out in support of my younger colleagues.

I must note, too, that in some ways, I find classism has impacted my work almost as much as racism. Euro-Americans are somewhat aware that the Unitarian Universalist Association vows to take (baby) steps toward dismantling racism but recognition of class assumptions proves more elusive. I remember a parent in one affluent congregation proudly telling me that she never says "no" to her toddler. I cannot imagine the world of privilege she is trying to instill in her child! A UUA staff person said he wanted to develop a financial literacy workshop for seminarians because students were assuming too much debt; did he want to limit the ministry to people flush with stocks and bank accounts?

Being *the* minister complicates how openly we can respond to racism and classism. Among "unprogrammed" Friends, everyone shares in ministry; there is no designated clergy. This is both a deep responsibility and a liberation. When, for example, I witness a classist or racist comment or action among Quakers, I can suggest we pause and examine it. I do not have to weigh how my words might impact the relationship between me, the ordained minister, and the UU congregation I serve. As Friends, we are equal partners.

In addition to my serving on regional boards of the American Friends Service Committee, the Quaker peace and justice arm, my three adult children inform my social change ministry. All are activists of some renown. Through them, I connect to contemporary movements ranging from queer liberation to livable cities to food justice to revolutionary arts to ending mass incarceration.

In my heart, I remain a Unitarian Universalist as well as a Quaker. I know, however, I will always experience tension within the UU fold. I am an outsider as an African American UU minister, as a person who has known both privilege and poverty. Yes, I thank the Association for inviting me to serve in a variety of capacities from committees to district and national boards to the Ministerial Fellowship Committee. I was among the initial group giving birth to DRUUMM (Diverse Revolutionary UU Multicultural Ministries), and it is empowering to discover BLUU (Black Lives of Unitarian Universalism). In such circles, I am nourished and strengthened. Retirement affords me the opportunity to preach in local UU churches, where I quickly settle into the familiar rhythm. It is a pleasure to craft a service—to study, write, weave in music and poetry, and connect in such a palpable and heartfelt way. I explore new interests from cello to batik and nurture deep ties with family and friends. Yes, there are candles of concern—many candles—but I also light a flame of joy for surviving, sometimes thriving, and witnessing the growing number of beautiful Black and brown faces who continue the journey. Ashe.

The Challenge of Change

REV. DR. MICHELLE BENTLEY

PRELIMINARY FELLOWSHIP (PARISH) 1986,
FULL FELLOWSHIP (PARISH) 1989,
FULL FELLOWSHIP (COMMUNITY) 1996

"Hello. Good morning." It was a probation officer for Project New Pride (PNP) on the other end of the line. I was serving as high school principal and assistant director for PNP, a partnership between Chicago's Better Boys' Foundation, Chicago Public Schools, and the Office of Juvenile Justice in Washington, D.C. PNP was a 1970s-era experimental program for males ages thirteen to eighteen who had been convicted of at least three serious crimes. These youth were now on their last chance to turn their lives around. They all came from Chicago. They were Asian, African American, Native American, Hispanic, and Caucasian. Our school, located in downtown Chicago, was neutral turf and served at any given time sixty students with highly qualified teachers, probation officers, and counselors. I often grappled with how best to help these young men, who were wandering in the wilderness. They needed more. I needed more knowledge because their issues were so wide and deep.

"One of our young boys was just arrested for a shooting and now sits at the Juvenile Detention at Cook County Jail," the probation officer told me.

"What? I'll be right there," I said. When I arrived, D and I cried together. D, only sixteen years old, a new father, and extremely book smart, had accompanied two older men attempting to rob the main post office in downtown Chicago. A security guard saw them, and a fight occurred. D tussled with the security guard, and the guard's gun

53

went off. The security guard, a Chicago policeman moonlighting, was pronounced dead at the scene. D was later tried as an adult and received a very long sentence.

Later that same week, I received another phone call, from my daughter's second-grade teacher, informing me that my seven-year-old had again been rushed by ambulance to La Rabida Children's Hospital for the Chronically and Terminally Ill, part of the University of Chicago Medical Center. I immediately dropped everything to be with Kya.

Kya was diagnosed at birth with SS, a severe form of sickle cell anemia, in which red blood cells turn sickle-shaped and can lodge in any joint or multiple joints, blocking oxygen and causing excruciating pain with possible damage to various organs. These episodes often result in hospitalization, sometimes several a month for weeks at a time.

The traumatic experience with D, an equally traumatic divorce, and caring for my chronically ill child all at once were overwhelming. I felt like I was also walking in the wilderness—numb and desperately trying to figure out how to take any time off from my job to care for my chronically ill child without being fired and risking my career.

I soon quit the PNP program and left the field of education. I went in search of growth, looking to delve deeper into the spirit.

In fact, I had been running from a different call for a while, but it was getting stronger. I'd been thinking about ministry. Often having the title Reverend gets people in power to take your call and engage with your concern in dialogue. Ministry gives one a platform from which to speak out, give witness, protest, ask questions. I needed that platform to turn my concerns into action.

I soon was employed at Garrett Theological School, where I took night theology classes with Rev. Dr. Henry Young, who later became a dear friend. I told him I loved studying theology but was not Christian and wanted to be somewhere studying and going deeper with those representing the diversity of world religions. He said, "I know just the person for you to talk with. He and I studied together at Boston University." I made an appointment with Rev. Dr. Gene Reeves, the president of Meadville Lombard Theological School, that day. My 2.5-hour meeting with him was life-changing. He introduced me to Unitarian Universalism, and we talked and talked.

Theologically, the Unitarian Universalism that Gene described felt like home. My journey into the world's religions and spirit started with the Baptists. From around age six through high school, my sister and I attended Trinity African Methodist Episcopal Church. We sang the glorious spirituals, something I also did while in Spelman's Choir and Atlanta University's Choir during my college years. In college, I was introduced to and studied Islam. Years later, I found the need for meditation and explored Nichiren Shoshu Buddhism, learned spiritual practices from the medicine woman Tillie Black Bear at the Rose Bud and Pine Ridge Lakota Nations, and climbed Bear Butte in South Dakota to talk with Gods. I visited with Ancestors and the Great Spirits of African religions and philosophies. I loved nature and, of course, the interdependent web of existence.

Gene described a Unitarian Universalism that incorporated women into its leadership. It was a community where I could bring the leadership I learned from my mother, my first teacher. My exposure to female leadership was deepened at Spelman College, deepened by my daughter's strength and courage, and deepened in my own positions as high school principal, national education consultant, and graduate school professor in education and inner-city studies. And I could bring my fierce womanism with me into Unitarian Universalism.

Gene told me about Unitarian Universalism's history and claim of social justice and activism. In the 1960s, I had participated fully in the activism of the times—learning, experiencing, and leading. I encountered the teachings of important activists, individuals like Jamil al-Amin (formerly known as H. Rap Brown), Stokely Carmichael, Malcolm X,

Rev. Dr. Martin Luther King Jr., Zora Neale Hurston, Karl Marx, Angela Y. Davis, and Spelman's Sisters in Blackness. I encountered dynamic organizations like SNCC, Nation of Islam, labor unions, the Socialist Party, the Communist Party, and Viet-Nam Vets & Deserters. I remember well the day Rev. Jesse Jackson came to Spelman's campus to tell us all about a jet with a full tank of gas waiting to transport its passengers to Memphis to participate in the Garbage Men's Strike, the poor people's fight. Many of us from HBCUs took him up on the offer. I marched with them on the first two of three marches in Memphis for the Poor People's Movement and Campaign. During the third Memphis march, Dr. King was assassinated. I wasn't able to attend that march, but I remember

I have always tried to bring the knowledge, skills, and passion I have learned from those who came before me.

vividly the vigils held on Atlanta HBCU campuses. I ushered the aisle where Robert F. Kennedy's family was seated during Dr. King's funeral on the campus of Morehouse, his alma mater. I have always tried to bring the knowledge, skills, and passion I have learned from those who came before me and I try to stay awoke: involved, marching, bringing care.

"Gene, all this sounds great," I told him, "but I have one concern: Can I fully bring my culture to Unitarian Universalism?"

Gene wanted to help me find my answers and sent me and Kya to Washington, DC, and New York to meet with three African American Unitarian Universalist ministers: Revs. David Eaton, Yvonne Seon, and Mark Morrison-Reed. The spirit of all three seemed revolutionary, and I felt at home. I also had the opportunity to meet with then UUA president Rev. Gene Pickett.

I had never heard of Unitarian Universalism before meeting Gene Reeves, and I was definitely not a joiner. But after the journey to meet

David, Yvonne, and Mark, I answered the call to ministry and joined in a huge way, as clergy.

In January of 1982, I was admitted into the University of Chicago's Divinity School and then automatically entered into Meadville, where I took UU history and ministry courses. While at the Divinity School, I studied with a diverse student body from a number of the world's religions. I remember well a presentation from young Professor Cornel West. Afterward, the African American folks continued discussion with Dr. West at my home.

Internship came fast. Kya and I chose the Community Church of New York (CCNY), where Rev. Bruce Southworth was the senior minister. I was his first intern and CCNY's first intern of color. CCNY was a diverse, progressive, socially active congregation and a partner in the UUA's Urban Church Coalition. It had an outstanding religious education program led by sister Marsha McBroom, the religious education director. One experience stands out: my coordination of the five-day New York leg of the 1983 USA Children of War-Torn Countries Tour, where fifteen students from Israel, Palestine, Harlem, El Salvador, Cambodia, Vietnam, Ireland, South Africa, Connecticut, and other places toured New York City to give witness to the suffering, violence, and death of loved ones from the wars. They told their stories of horror, survival, and love and asked for world peace.

During one of Kya's hospitalizations at La Rabida Children's Hospital, I wrote a proposal to start a chaplaincy program there. The proposal was funded and I provided s ix hours a week visiting doctors, nurses, staff, and patients, and I facilitated a parents' group. I maintained this chaplaincy position alongside my seminary work and work-study for three years.

There is a gospel song with this lyric: "May not come when you want but comes right on time." My last year in seminary, I met Ray Bentley at Mr. G's, a local grocery store. He was raised Catholic and thought it was interesting that I was studying to be a minister and buying a six-pack of beer for the famous 1986 Chicago Bears Superbowl game. A year and half later, we married and two years after that, Michael was born.

In 1986, there were only three ordained women Unitarian Universalists of African descent: Yvonne Seon, Adele Smith-Penniman, and me. According to Rev. Rose Eddington's D.Min dissertation, "In 1968, in the UUA, there were eight white female ministers and eight African American ministers, all male. In 1998, out of 1,333 total clergy, there were approximately 470 white female clergy, which represented 35 percent of the total ministry, and 32 ministers of color, with twenty of those of African descent (fourteen male and seven female)."

When I was right out of seminary, the UUA district executive and two UU ministers wrote a grant, without my input, for me to organize two new and diverse church starts in three years. I did—North River Unitarian Universalist and South Loop Unitarian Universalist. Rev. Mel Hoover came and officially blessed them, and they were both recognized at General Assemblies as fully fledged Unitarian Universalist congregations. Several years later, however, the UUA flatly stated that the new church starts organized by African American ministers had failed. But our congregations were special and had in fact succeeded in spite of severely insufficient funding and low expectations. The new starts I was ordered to organize were pejoratively designed to give African American ministers jobs. I was told, "Start two churches in three years or you're opting out of the ministry because that's the only employment open to you." We did not fail. The denomination failed us.

In the third year of my new church starts, I heard of a major substance abuse program, BRASS (Behavior, Research, and Action in the Social Sciences), moving into my community. Within a week, I sent a proposal to the executive director for a spiritual/therapeutic component, including religious education classes and pastoral care. A month later, she called me to say that my proposal was exactly what she had been hoping for. It was the first such component to a treatment program in Illinois. I turned my two new church starts over to other ministers and began doing the type of ministry I always wanted to do, full-time community ministry. I had the wonderful opportunity to be with people struggling with cocaine, heroin/methadone, and alcohol addictions. BRASS also had a Prevention and Youth program and Essence House for Women, a residential treatment program. I've taken several courses on addiction and continue to mentor several women from BRASS. I am godmother to the daughter of one former resident. I helped but I also learned a great deal from the people at BRASS.

While my BRASS chaplaincy was full time, I was also called as the quarter-time associate minister for social action at First Unitarian Church of Chicago. A couple of years later, as BRASS's state funding ended for the chaplaincy program, First Unitarian called me to be their full-time interim minister. We did much, and we grew as a congregation. I particularly remember celebrating the election of Brother Nelson Mandela with the larger community.

First Unitarian Society of Chicago was and is my home church. Rev. Duke Gray took me under his wing early and made me his student minister, and later the congregation called me to become the youth and college youth director. The congregation was diverse, progressive, and part of the Urban Church Coalition, with wonderfully skilled, supportive, and talented female lay leaders. These women were like aunts and sisters to me and Kya—Dr. Norman (Alex) Poinsett, Judge R. Morgan Hamilton (my son's godmother), Betty Holcomb, Grace Latibeaudiere-Williams, Evelyn Johnson, Mary Lee Greenlee, Vivian Burns, Madeira Myricks, Kenny James, Vivian Burns, Aqui Yasuaki, Polly (Randy) Vaughn, and others. They took such good care of us. It also helped that my sister Nikki and her family lived in the neighborhood and our parents lived only an hour away in our childhood home. My parents and other family members attended and pledged financial support at every church I served.

Theologian James Luther Adams wrote, "Every personal problem is a social problem and every social problem is a personal problem." This maxim lies at the core of my theology. That's why I've spent half my ministry as a community minister and half in a parish that always worked in and with the community creating seven-day-a-week programming for families. While I was doing my chaplaincy at BRASS, Unitarian Universalist ministry students were being told by denominational leadership and seminaries that if they wanted to do community ministry, they would pretty much have to figure it all out on their own. But Meadville Lombard faculty worked with other community ministers to make final fellowship in community ministry possible, and several of us were grandparented in. I also had a final fellowship in parish ministry.

After three years as associate and then interim minister at First Unitarian, Meadville Lombard president Rev. Dr. Spencer Lavan and faculty called me and I walked across the street to serve for five years as dean of students, the first faculty member who was African American or a person of color there. My time as faculty when there were more students of color at the school than ever before was both wonderful and challenging. My 1998 D.Min. dissertation, "The White Face of Theological Education: A Case Study of Movement to Antiracist, Multicultural Theological Education," documents much of my multicultural work, which was again beyond the normal responsibilities of the dean of students and ministry instructor. My time at Meadville Lombard culminated in my designing and implementing an antiracism conference with faculty from Meadville Lombard and Starr King Theological School and denominational leaders and activists.

Five years later, I returned to inner city ministry at Third Unitarian Universalist Church on Chicago's West Side. Professor Betty Jean Harris, the Board chair, was a strong and excellent leader, and she and Rev. Dr. Penny Allderdice, the assistant minister, helped make my time at Third UU Church special. The congregation grew in its diversity with members of African descent and other people and families of color, LGBTQ and straight and cisgender people, and did important work: we shut down two crack houses in the surrounding community, built a seven-day-a-week church with gardening, registered people to vote, delivered Thanksgiving baskets, developed our Harriet Tubman House for HIV education and a food pantry, and more. Again, I could not have made it through without family and special women: Nikki and Edwina Whittingham, Vivian Jones, Kimry Lee, Rolanda Webb, Karen Latham-Williams, Theresa Riley, and many others. A friend of Third UU Church was the first African American public defender in Chicago and Cook County, Randolph Stone. He and another church friend, Dr. Alvin Hill, coordinator of the Cook County Public Defender's Sentencing Advocacy Program, invited me to become an expert consultant. I volunteered as the only chaplain to serve those awaiting trial for murder. I worked in maximum security jail divisions to help mitigate the sentences of men who were charged with multiple rapes and murders, and with young girls who were charged with killing their babies. I am still working in Religious Services at the infamous county jail.

Such ministry (hospital, substance abuse, prison, gangs) isn't for the meek. It brings you up close to horrific childhood stories; mental illness of individuals, families, and the larger communities; and the inner workings of the industrial prison complex, the medical system, and the industrial drugs and alcohol complex, with each institution exhibiting racial bias and racist practices and causing great pain and suffering. I bore witness to our African American generational suffering and went deeper into psychopathology and theology to learn how to see both the suffering and divine sparks in people and offer balm, to bring people together and offer love, hope, and support. To do community or parish ministry, you have to go where the pain is, be agile, know how to write grants and proposals, find your niche, make contacts, know how to organize, and not be afraid because you have faith in yourself, you have done the work with experience, and walk a path with heart knowing your god/ higher power is walking with you and has your back. Each individual I served was in great need of pastoral care, compassion, and advocacy. Each institution was in need of reform to be just and equitable.

My five years at Third UU Church ended in joy and pain, and then I went to the Unitarian Universalist Association. I interviewed with UUA president Rev. Bill Sinkford and executive vice president Kay Montgomery from the meditation garden at a hospital in Memphis, Tennessee, where Kya was hospitalized in the ICU. The interview went well, and I then served the UUA as director of professional development in the Department of Ministry and Leadership with Rev. David Hubner, where I did a great deal: I oversaw the continuing education process, guided troubled ministries, served on the Ministerial Fellowship Committee, oversaw ministerial final fellowship, administered the Borden Sermon Award, lectured at Ministry Professional Days, endorsed military chaplains, and more.

Five years later, I retired from the Unitarian Universalist Association but began a three-year stint working at Grand Boulevard Safety Net Program, a federal and citywide funded program to coordinate and supervise former gang leaders in their outreach to youth. The gangs included Chicago Black Disciples, Black Gangster Disciples, Mickey D-Disciples, and Black Stone Rangers.

Perhaps to make ministry a less lonely path, I facilitated monthly meetings and student programs with African American faculty from the other local seminaries (Presbyterian, Catholic, Lutheran, Methodist, and the University of Chicago Divinity School, which is nonsectarian). I created and directed the Sankofa Archive for Ministers and Laity of Color to recognize and highlight our work and our stories and our ways of being in this world, to make sure we would no longer be left out of UU stories and history. Taquiena Boston, then the director of the UUA's Identity-Based Ministries Office, and I started the Finding

Our Way Home annual retreat for African American clergy in the early 2000s. I created annual General Assembly gatherings for and in support of African American female clergy and the newly ordained, and seminarians because our contributions were often left out of events sponsored by white female clergy.

I would be remiss not to include in this chapter my unofficial ministry with All Souls Unitarian Universalist Fellowship, founded by one of our denomination's first African American ministers, Rev. Lewis Allen McGee. (Rev. McGee was ordained in the AME Church in 1917 and served as a U.S. Army chaplain in 1918 and from 1943 to 1945. He was the first African American minister to serve a white church and a Meadville Lombard 1948 graduate.) The All Souls congregation is where many well-known Chicago artists and educators attended and received their spiritual liberal teachings. Many of these same individuals helped elect Chicago's first Black mayor, Harold Washington. All members at All Souls were very supportive of me and my ministry, people like Thelma Toussaint, Judge Marion Perkins, Darrell Phillips, Virginia Bennett, Eric and Eleanor Graham, and Geneva Bishop. I am grateful for their care, support, and contributions.

Right out of seminary, I thoroughly enjoyed serving as interim minister at Park Forrest Unitarian Universalist Church of the South Suburbs. Also, as the associate minister at the historic Peoples' Church on Chicago's North Side, later renamed the Preston Bradley Center. This had been a joint United Church of Christ and Unitarian Universalist congregation. I was the last Unitarian Universalist minister to serve there.

I fondly remember marrying my dear friends the day after Chicago passed the marriage equality ruling. I remember the wedding in the cemetery under the weeping willow on Halloween. I remember Sharon, who committed suicide the day after telling me she was gay. I remember performing two holy union ceremonies on the Jerry Springer Show, a couple years before the show truly went off the rails. And I remember with a smile the scores of ordination sermons preached and parish interns supervised.

Today, my life seems to be turning full circle. I'm facilitating a group for women age sixty and older. "Our Golden Years," some call them. Incidentally, "The Challenge of Change" was the title of my first and last sermons preached in my forty plus years of ministry. All those years have been served in the same district and the same town. I have been able to take care of and be with my husband, children, grandchildren, sister and her family, parents, and friends throughout my ministry. I have gotten to be a big part of several progressive congregations with many special, unique, and gifted Unitarian Universalists of African descent and many people of all races, ethnicities, and religious beliefs.

Ministry has been very rewarding for me and saved my life. It has given me the opportunity to learn and grow, find joy, and be of service to people from many walks of life.

Not by Ourselves Alone

REV. MARJORIE BOWENS-WHEATLEY
PRELIMINARY FELLOWSHIP (PARISH) 1994, FULL FELLOWSHIP (PARISH) 1997, PRELIMINARY FELLOWSHIP (RELIGIOUS EDUCATION) 2002, DIED 2006

Homily delivered March 8, 2002, at the Unitarian Universalist Ministers Convocation in Birmingham, Alabama

In the late 1970s through the mid-1980s, I was living in Washington, D.C, working as a journalist and public television producer. I had chosen a profession in the news media because I wanted people to have the option of a different spin on the news of the corporate monopolies. I wanted to do stories so compelling that people might not only be inspired, but actually feel compelled to act.

Some of you will recall that the 1980s was a time when car jackings were a regular occurrence in some urban areas, and I was out covering such a story. An African American woman about my age (I was 35 or 36 at the time) was filling up her car with gasoline, and in the flash of an eye, a moment when she had turned away, someone had driven off not only with her car, but with her eight-year-old daughter. Now I must tell you that I too had a daughter, so I had a deep identification with this woman.

When I arrived on the scene, there were at least five radio and television stations that had set up their equipment, and four reporters had microphones in her face. I looked around at my camera man, who was about to join the mob, and I looked at the woman. She was visibly and understandably upset, speaking in a soft voice, but not all of her sentences were complete or coherent. I made my way closer to her, all the time monitoring the pace of my crew's set-up. As other reporters probed her with questions, I placed my hand in hers. I remember thinking to myself, *Why don't they leave her alone?* And then there was this sudden awareness that *I* was one of them. They were my fellow reporters. And yet I knew that the last thing she needed was a gang of microphones in her face. In a flash, I remembered the words of one of my professors who, emphasizing that television news had to have pictures to maintain its dramatic focus, had said to the class "keep the camera rolling until you make them cry."

What this woman needed was someone to talk to about her troubles, someone to console her, someone with whom she could let out all her fears—without fear of exploitation, someone to tell her "it's gonna be alright." And when she grasped onto my hand for what seemed like dear life, I knew that I couldn't do the story, that I couldn't keep the camera rolling.

I begged my fellow reporters to give her some breathing room, and she must have sensed that I had her interest at heart, because as I quietly guided her away from the crowd and toward my station's van, she did not resist. Eventually, the microphones and the reporters disappeared, audiotape and videotape in hand for the evening news. The woman had held back the tears from the cameras, but within moments, she was weeping incessantly. As we sat waiting for a family member to arrive, I tried to comfort her between the tears as she told me bits and pieces of the story—without camera, without microphone. And when we parted, I said to her, "Keep the faith. You *will* see your daughter again." And indeed, she did.

I could not get this woman out of my mind for the rest of the day, and when I went home that evening, it became really clear to me why. My values had gotten confused. I had had a long period of absence from churches, and so at the time, I didn't have the religious language to name what had happened with the woman at the gas station. I didn't realize until much later that I was doing pastoral ministry. The person behind the story had become more important to me than getting the story. And I knew that I could no longer be a reporter, at least not *that kind* of reporter. I knew that I would have to leave the media. I remained one more year at the television station to finish the documentary that I had already begun. I had been an activist, involved in social justice work. With this, along with a deep need and longing for reconnection with a faith community, I found my way to All Souls Church in Washington, DC.

When I saw an announcement on the church bulletin board of a job opening at the Unitarian Universalist Service Committee, there was no doubt in my mind. I had to work in a place where I could align my values with my work. And it wasn't long—perhaps a few months—before I was moving to Boston to live and nurture my faith, and to put my faith into action.

At the Service Committee, and later at the Veatch Program, I began to understand justice work as ministry. But it wasn't until I was in theological school

> *I had to work in a place where I could align my values with my work.*

that I found a definition of faith that made sense to me. It is gaining confidence through relating to others that there is sustaining grace in the universe, a power beyond ourselves that holds us, and that we experience this power through our relationships with others and they with us.

In other words, faith is relational.

I now understood that the work I had done with the woman at the gas station might have been important in nurturing her faith as well as my own. For me, it was a turning point—an experience that helped to clarify my values, test the profession of journalism in a new way, and inform my faith, which was not fully coherent.

I answered the call, and here I am, still nurturing my faith.

Why I Have Stayed

REV. DR. KRISTEN L. HARPER
PRELIMINARY FELLOWSHIP 1999, FULL FELLOWSHIP 2002

In one sense, I didn't choose Unitarian Universalism. I was adopted at eighteen months into a Unitarian Universalist family. The Principles and Purposes were not adopted until I was a teenager, but the First Congregational Unitarian Church of Harvard, Massachusetts, taught me the values of love, searching for the truth in freedom, speaking the truth in love, and service to humanity. However, the congregation also embraced the idea that they didn't "see color" and because I refused to deny my color and I was clearly not white, I was invisible to them and pretty much ignored by everyone except the children's choir and Christmas pageant director. I remember the comments directed toward me when I was an angel in the Christmas pageant. The director wanted me in front as I could dance and knew the steps, but some of the other mothers wanted me in the back because they said the "balance" was off. I am not sure how one balances seven little white girls with one little Black girl, but I ended up in the back row.

I hated Sunday school because few of the kids would play with me and the teacher ignored me altogether. The only parts I enjoyed were the Bible stories that the teacher would share and have us talk about. I ended up attending more of the Sunday services, and as long as I sat quietly, no one paid attention. Rev. Malcolm Sutherland was a strong and powerful presence in the pulpit, and I enjoyed listening to him talk about different justice issues and about the human Jesus who tried to change the lives of the least of these.

As I got older, I tried to join the youth group and regional events. My brother Jamie, who was blond and blue-eyed, was very popular, but I was ostracized and often sat alone or wandered outside. I continued to attend church, and although I babysat many of the church members' children and gardened in their yards, when it came time to ask for Church sponsorship, a requirement for Unitarian Universalist ministry, the members of the Board said no one really knew who I was. I had been invisible.

During two different periods of my life, I chose to attend another church, and in both cases, I loved the music and hated the dogma and doctrine. I was raised to question any truth blithely stated that I didn't understand, that didn't fit with my experience, that couldn't be proven, that just didn't feel right. I was raised to believe that we must participate in bending the arc of the universe toward justice. I believed that and didn't think prayer alone would save anyone. I was raised to believe that all faith traditions had truths and insights that could help humanity live more gently with ourselves, one another, and the earth. And I believed all faith traditions were created by a deeply flawed humanity that has yet to fully come to terms with its destructive and oppressive power. I could not pledge my allegiance to Christianity or to my birth religion of Judaism or even Buddhism. I was a Unitarian Universalist.

During my second sojourn from our faith, I was looking to have greater connection with the Black community. I was tired of being the only or one of only two people of color at a UU gathering. And frankly, I was tired of going to UU gatherings during which I was made to feel invisible or intruding on a special club I was not cool enough to belong to—the "White Club." I attended an American Baptist Church for a year and an African Methodist Episcopal Church twice. It was wonderful to be surrounded by people who looked like me, but I was so disturbed by the theological justification for discriminating against others because of who they loved that I left in a huff. But before I stormed out, I tried for a year to connect to a being that seemed not to like Black people very much and allowed tremendous suffering to occur all over the world. I was a humanist at heart.

When I graduated from college, I had no idea what I wanted to do. Although a friend had jokingly said I should be a minister as I was always "preaching" about issues of justice, it wasn't an idea that stuck in my head. I had been volunteering with women who were HIV positive and sharing my spiritual grounding with them to counteract the oppressive cultural idea that they were being punished by God. Mostly I spent time listening to the challenges and obstacles of poverty, racism, sexualization, and abuse they had been trying to overcome all their lives and marveled at the joy and gratitude many of them had for the smallest of things. I tried to be present to their living and not afraid to touch them as they died of AIDS.

I have told the story of how I went to work at the UUA as a moment of grace. I had applied to be a social worker, was accepted by the Massachusetts Department of Social Service, and then told to wait to be placed in an office. As the wait turned into months, I decided to apply for a position at the Unitarian Universalist Association as an administrative assistant to Jacqui James, the director of the Office of Worship and Diversity Resources. The day I was hired at the UUA, I came home and found a message on my answering machine placing me at the Jamaica Plain office of the Department of Social Services. I decided to work for the UUA instead.

I was hired to complete *Between the Lines: Notes to Singing the Living Tradition* and stayed on to work with Jacqui on *Weaving the Fabric of Diversity*, the second edition of *Black Pioneers in a White Denomination*, and other resources for Unitarian Universalist ministers and congregations. I was asked to preach a couple of times at UU congregations due to my work as a Beyond Categorical Thinking workshop leader, a program on avoiding bias in the search process, but still I felt no call to the ministry. Although a couple UUA staff members suggested I check ministry out, it wasn't until a young female seminarian came to a meeting of the African American Unitarian Universalist Ministries group that I was persuaded to take a leap of faith into ministry. Danielle Gladd was one of the most dynamic young women I had ever met. She was seven months younger than I, smart, and full of spirit, and she drew me toward her. We were both raised Unitarian Universalists in white families. We were both biracial, comfortable in our Black identities, and comfortable in both predominantly white settings and settings with all people of color. We also both had the experience of not feeling as if we completely belonged anywhere. When we met, we realized we belonged with each other. Danielle and I later gathered together other multiracial and transracially adopted youth and young adults for community and identity development.

Although I was aware that Unitarian Universalism was a predominantly white religious Association, I was not prepared for the racism I experienced beginning in seminary. From being called a quota filler, to being maced, to being told I didn't belong, it was three and a half years of being under attack by people who were supposed to be my colleagues, my professors, members of my community of faith. Danielle refused to accept the racism quietly and demanded her right to be there. She and I reached out to other Black ministers and UUA staff for help but were told not to be so intimidating, not to make waves, that we were pioneers and pioneers should expect hardship and suffering. Danielle ignored this advice and the system could not withstand her demands for justice and she was pushed out. I wanted to go with her, but she insisted I stay and make my mark.

My internship at the Community Church of New York was another time of grace. The community was, I believe, 35 percent Black and had been working on dismantling their racism for ninety years, since Rev. John Haynes Holmes intentionally worked to integrate its membership. Rev. Bruce Southworth, my internship supervisor, worked with me on both my ministerial development and my identity development through thoughtful questioning and prodding, acknowledging the racial challenges I would face from white communities and communities of color, and working on strengthening my sense of worth and dignity.

The community of Black women at Community Church of New York was a diverse group of African American, Caribbean American, African, and West Indian women. They demonstrated solidarity alongside an appreciation of the multiplicities of cultures within their cohort. They were incredibly intelligent, strong, spiritually deep women who mentored and supported me in a quiet, non-domineering manner— except to insist I not dred my hair, which I had been considering. They gave me the opportunity to minister to them and to learn from them at the same time. Dr. Janice Marie Johnson and Rev. Hope Johnson, two of the then members, were instrumental in helping me develop my sense of self as a minister and providing examples of Black women who fully embraced who they were and remained comfortable in any community in which they found themselves.

During my final year at Meadville Lombard Theological School, I wrote my doctoral dissertation about the six women of African descent who had preceded me into Unitarian Universalist ministry: Yvonne Seon, Adele Smith-Penniman, Michelle Bentley, Toni Vincent, Marjorie Bowens-Wheatley, and Alma Faith Crawford. Today it is hard to believe that in 1999, I was only the seventh Black woman ordained and fellowshipped in our faith. Rev. Shana Lynngood was fellowshipped the same year that I was, but ordained later. I had lived with Alma in Jamaica Plain, Massachusetts, the summer before I left for seminary and attended the church she served in Roxbury, filling in when she needed me. Michelle was the dean of students at Meadville Lombard Theological School for three of the years I attended, and Marjorie was the associate minister at Community Church of New York while I was an intern. They all represented very different models for me about how to be a Black woman in our faith.

One of the things I learned while researching about Black women's rise in our ministry was that for many years, they were not encouraged to enter the settlement process as sole or senior ministers. Instead they were encouraged to start new congregations or to be associates or assistants. I entered the search process in the winter of 1999 with no precedent to follow. I applied to and was called to serve the Unitarian Universalist Society of the Daytona Beach Area in Ormond Beach, Florida. Adele Smith-Penniman also entered search that year and was called to the First Congregational Parish Unitarian in Petersham, Massachusetts.

The three years I spent in Ormond Beach were tremendous learning years but not happy ones. My office administrator announced to me that she did not like Black people, accused me of stealing to members of the congregation, and reported me to the IRS. Thankfully, there was nothing to report. She called me on almost every day off and would tell members she didn't know where I was even though I wrote my schedule on her calendar. The congregational leadership refused to do anything about her harassment and generally avoided all conflict. During my first year, there was so much bullying during our board meetings that I would leave meetings and eventually have to pull my car over on my way home to throw up. Although I was approached by other congregations to apply for their open ministerial positions, I was determined to stay for the agreed upon three to five years.

When I arrived in Ormond, the church had just completed the feasibility study for a capital campaign to build a new church complex. Together we raised the money, and a Spanish-style new building was built on the same site. The congregation grew, and we got involved as founding members of Fighting Against Injustice Towards Harmony (FAITH), a Volusia County interfaith, multiracial organization that worked on providing drug treatment in jails, eliminating drug hot spots in Daytona Beach, and updating the school curricula for middle schoolers. We held dialogues with the NAACP on race relations, and we reached out to the local synagogue to build relationships. I trained as a police chaplain and walked the streets during Black College Reunion to ensure the safety of the college students on spring break.

One of the most amazing and memorable aspects of my time with the Ormond congregation, which was nearly 80 percent seniors over seventy, was that the majority of the members invited me into their lives and shared their joys and challenges. They allowed me to minister to them in their times of distress and to walk with them as they died. I was forty years younger than most of them and Black, but they were hungry for loving connections and welcomed my service with appreciation. They joined me in the community in very large numbers to do the work of justice and were open to understanding the effects of racism on communities of color. However, they were unable to see or address the overt racism of their office administrator and some of the members.

At General Assembly in 2001, I was standing outside the convention center when Rev. Gene Pickett came up to me and started up a conversation. He asked me how it was going in Florida, and I told him it wasn't great. Rev. Pickett talked to me about a congregation in Massachusetts where he had been a member and said that they were now in search for a new minister. I remember his exact words, "I believe they're ready for a Black woman minister." I decided to check them out online. What I remember most about their website was the picture of their familiar New England church and steeple and their covenant, which was similar to the one I grew up reciting:

Love is the doctrine of this church. The quest for truth is its sacrament and service is its prayer. To dwell together in peace, to seek knowledge in freedom, to serve humanity in fellowship, to the end that all souls shall grow into harmony with the divine, thus do we covenant together.

I was interested.

Another struggle I had in Florida was that although I was a humanist, I was a spiritual humanist. The vocal members of the Unitarian Universalist Church of the Daytona Beach Area were more atheistic and had more bruises about religious language than I was comfortable with. I had mentioned God in one of my first sermons and a member yelled out, "We don't believe in God!" I felt that the secular humanism embraced by some in Ormond Beach espoused an individualism that allowed for people to think more about their own inherent worth and dignity than others'. There was not a strong sense of accountability to one another's feelings and diverse perspectives.

For a few years, I had described myself using Rev. William Jones' term, *a humano-centric-theist*, or a panentheist. I was still trying to find a way to clearly express my theology. I didn't believe in an anthropomorphic deity, but I did believe that whatever was divine, sacred, holy became more potent when we moved together. I now most often describe myself as a spiritual humanist, and if someone is interested, I then explain, "I believe that which we call God—the energetic force of love and creation in the universe—is within us and around us, connecting us and empowering us as we move toward one another and into the world."

Theologically I felt that I could be a good match with the Unitarian Church of Barnstable, Massachusetts, which met most of the requirements on my list. Barnstable felt different from Ormond Beach from the beginning, with a good mix of theological points of view and tolerance for spiritual language, although somewhat Christian-shy. Their record of working on racial justice went back to the 1960s, when they were instrumental in organizing housing, food, clothing, and employment during the Reverse Freedom Rides. They had a handful of members of color and had the beginnings of a multiracial religious education program.

I always say that I knew I would accept an offer of a call to Barnstable when I saw the children and youth center. Yes, it was in the basement, but on the ceiling was a huge dreamcatcher; on the walls were pictures of Black women dancing. In addition, there were Black and brown angel dolls, posters of children from all around the world holding hands, and books featuring Asians and Indigenous people. I knew I wanted to work with whoever the person was who was trying to create a positive multicultural environment.

Although deer sullivan, the amazing, forward-thinking, creative, deeply spiritual director of religious education left after five years, she returned to be our director of lifespan religious education in 2017. As one of the most earth-grounded and sky-flying people I know, deer has taught me so much in ministry. For the entire first year we worked together, every time she suggested something I thought "no" but said "yes!" The religious education program consisted of sixty strong, happy, and engaged children. The program grew and my late husband, Jay, and I were trained as Our Whole Lives (OWL) facilitators and began leading OWL every other year. We grew a youth group and worked with many amazing youth.

I arrived at the Unitarian Church of Barnstable during the big push for marriage equality in Massachusetts. Two of the plaintiffs in the legal battle, Gloria and Linda Bailey-Davies, were members of First Parish Brewster, Unitarian Universalist, just twenty minutes down the road from us. First Parish Brewster mobilized in the Lower Cape, we mobilized in the Mid-Cape, and Falmouth mobilized in the Upper Cape. With the local interfaith group, we organized hundreds of people into the Cape Cod Community College auditorium to explain why we supported marriage equality and we invited their support. We sent bus after bus of Unitarian Universalists to Boston to march and pressure the legislature to legalize marriage equality.

Even as I helped organize community rallies and education forums, even as I marched and wrote letters, even as I argued against civil unions and for full marriage rights, even then I knew it wasn't really about same-sex marriage. It was about marriage itself. It was all about love. If my sister's love could not be recognized legally, if Megan and Carla could not be married with all the federal and state protections, what did it say about my marriage? What did it say about me? How was I more deserving of this basic right than my sister?

Two years later, on May 16, 2004, as Carla, Megan, and I stood for hours in line at the Cambridge clerk's office in order to apply for one of the first marriage licenses issued to same-sex couples, I began to smile. There was so much excitement and joy radiating all around me and the talk of wedding plans and ceremonial rituals made me smile. I smiled for my sister and my sister-in-law; I smiled for all the same-sex couples whose love and commitments were now being recognized by law; but mostly I smiled that finally my marriage was legitimate. During the twenty-one years I have been a minister, I have helped bury nearly 150 people. I have married almost a hundred couples and dedicated dozens of children. But I can think of nothing more satisfying than standing in front of my sister and her wife and pronouncing them "joined in marriage."

Because I had struggled so much with racism in my first called position, I rarely spoke about it when I first came to Barnstable. That doesn't mean there was no racism—like the time an eighty-year-old member claimed I battered her and people did not believe me or my witnesses that I was nothing but kind to her; like the members who primarily talked with me about race issues or about the Black people they knew; like the members who said I sounded angry whenever I did talk about the racism I experienced; like the people who thought I must be from the city or commented on how articulate I am. Once a member who liked to talk about all the Black people she had worked with described an incident when she saw a Black man who looked like my husband running out from an alley with blood all over him. She said he had clearly been beaten and reveled in the telling of his injuries and how her parents instructed her to roll up the windows.

There have been times when I have been introduced as "our Black minister," or members have been introduced as "people who bring diversity to the congregation." But the most common form of racism is the denial that it even exists. White members have gone to great lengths to excuse or explain away the racism I and members of color experience in the church and in the community: we "misunderstood," are "too sensitive," are "seeing things that aren't there." It was even suggested that we have a conversation to debate whether or not an incident was actually racist.

Unfortunately, because I needed to work and there was no place to put the pain, anger, humiliation, and betrayal I felt, depression and anxiety soon became my daily companions. I took my shame out on myself, and there were many times I did not know if I could continue as a minister. But then someone would get sick, someone would die, someone would have a crisis, someone would need me, and I would open my broken heart again and again in the service of others.

> *White members have gone to great lengths to excuse or explain away the racism I and members of color experience in the church and in the community: we "misunderstood," are "too sensitive," are "seeing things that aren't there."*

The most surprising and disappointing aspect of Unitarian Universalist ministry has been the racism of my white colleagues. When I first began ministry, I was asked by a colleague if she could put my picture on the wall of her church so her members could see that there are Black Unitarian Universalists. I had to listen at different chapter meetings as white colleagues competed with one another about the number of "African American" members they had. Colleagues have touched my hair without permission, asked me to park their cars, and called me by another Black woman's name and then gotten irritated when I corrected their mistake.

Once when I preached at a colleague's church, they put another Black woman's photo on the order of service. I have been ignored and made invisible by colleagues stepping in front of me to get service from other colleagues. Colleagues have interrupted services I was leading for them to "correct" a ritual I was performing. I have been told by white colleagues that they know more about the experience of racism than I do because they marched with Rev. Dr. Martin Luther King Jr. and worked with Bishop Desmond Tutu. Colleagues think nothing of interrupting, dismissing, or challenging me, or ignoring my requests. Sometimes when I have responded to questions, some colleagues have ignored my answer in favor of the same answer from a white colleague. I have been reprimanded and called intimidating for talking about the racism I have experienced within collegial settings and told I must "assume good will." I have been told that the Unitarian Universalist Minister's Association is not interested in repairing their relationship with me and would rather focus on "collective liberation" instead.

So the question that must be answered is why stay? Why stay in a faith that does not want me, in a system that rejects who I am. I could say that it is because Unitarian Universalism needs me; it needs people of color who are willing to take the abuse and remain at the table. But I am no martyr and I do not believe in sacrificial theology. I could honestly say it is because I was raised a Unitarian Universalist and there is no other place, no other faith tradition in which I would fit, and that would be true.

Part of the reason I have been able to stay as long as I have is my friendship with Rev. Dr. Abhi Janamanchi and his wife, Lalitha Janamanchi. They have been my main support, particularly after the death of Danielle Gladd, who died from pancreatic cancer in 2018. I met Abhi and Lalitha in my first year of seminary, and we wove a friendship as Lalitha cooked for me weekly and they both listened to me and shared with me and integrated me and my husband Jay into their family. We have been there for one another in the worst of times and in the best of times. But even that would not have been enough to keep me in the UU ministry.

The main reason I have stayed, the thing that has kept me at it all these years, is that I cannot think of anything I would rather do. There are moments in ministry that cannot be replicated in any other work—moments like when a member must decide whether or not to take their son off life support and they turn to you to help them make a decision that reflects their values and their hearts, moments when you have spent a year walking with a member through the grief of losing her husband and you see her begin to live again, moments when you get to hold a newborn baby or hold the hand of someone who is dying, moments when you get to change one mind about the rights of transgender people, moments when you get to be prophetic, moments when a single phone call helps a person understand their humanity and their worth, moments when your hug is the only touch a person has all week, moments when your listening can change the course of a person's life. There are moments in this work when the freedom, acceptance, and love of this faith can actually save lives.

Has all this been worth the trauma and heartbreak that racism has caused for me? I don't know the answer to that question. What I do know is that it has given my life meaning and purpose and for that I am grateful.

A Profession of Faith

REV. ANGELA M. DAVIS
PRELIMINARY FELLOWSHIP 2002, DIED 2003

Rev. Davis wrote the profession of faith from which the following is excerpted for her application to the Unitarian Universalist Association's Ministerial Fellowship Committee.

I believe in God, a God of love, power, and grace who looks like me and every other gift here on earth and anywhere else in the Universe! She is a gracious, loving, kind God. She is the God of my mother Ella, my grandmother Elizabeth, and my great grandmother Maria. I am their child and belong to them, as they are God's children and belong to her. I am a child of God ... It is my humble contribution to this extraordinary faith tradition. I recognize its frailties and challenges. I only ask to be given an opportunity to serve as I can, to share what I have, to be seen as "I am."

Why I Want to Be a UU Minister

I ask myself that question too! I want to be an ordained UU minister because I feel called by the God of my faith to formally do her work. Every opportunity and each experience in my life has prepared me to work, speak, and live a theology, UU theology, that affirms the right to "be as is" in the world.

My distilled experiences, formal and informal religious education, and the way in which I perceive the divine encompass the power of love.

My familial religious background is traditional, Southern Baptist and African Methodist Episcopal. However, I experienced religion through many unique, nontraditional demonstrations of faith. The two women whom I consider my parents, my great grandmother and mother, both demonstrated great faith in God, the power of prayer, and the infinite possibilities that life has to offer. Yet neither felt compelled to attend a church on a regular basis. Both women felt strongly that faith was *not* demonstrated in what one wears on Sunday but how one lives Monday through Saturday. In order to meet enrollment requirements, I attended Catholic Church for three years between the ages of four and seven. By age nine, my father had become a minister in the Southern Baptist tradition. Sunday services in my father's church were my most prolonged and significant experience in a "traditional" religious environment.

Every opportunity and each experience in my life has prepared me to work, speak, and live a theology, UU theology, that affirms the right to "be as is" in the world.

Thinking much like an investigative reporter, I listened and learned the craft of ministry without hearing the message of the service. Many Sunday evenings, I questioned my mother about my father's sermons. I would relate to my mother the discrepancies between the messenger and the message. Then I asked the real question, "How can a God who created the flowers in our garden, Grandma, and you be vengeful and seek retribution on the people 'He' put on this earth?" I have never understood how the God I learned about from Mom and Grandma could be the same God preached about on Sunday in my father's church.

I began to realize early in life that God was not the same for every individual or every denomination. In addition to my AME, Baptist, and Catholic experiences, three very significant people in my life were religious and cultural Jews. In the mind of a nine-year-old, I surmised that God was as I had learned, everywhere, represented in every part of life and spoke in a "gazillion" different languages!

I bring these thoughts, the breadth of my experiences, and passion for justice to ministry. However, I must state clearly that I chose to candidate for this Ministry in response to a strong spiritual call to perform ethical, just, faith-based work in the world in which I live.

This Faith Is Mine

REV. DR. HOPE JOHNSON

PRELIMINARY FELLOWSHIP 2002,
FULL FELLOWSHIP 2005, DIED 2020

When I first heard about the Black Lives Matter movement, I was all over it. All excited that there was finally a moment in time—a moment in *my lifetime* when the focus was on me. What's not to love? Yes, it was time for something palpably positive to be done for people who look like me. The focus was on protecting my people from violence, police brutality, racial profiling, unjust incarceration—and so much more . . .

Co-founders Patrisse Cullors, Opal Tometi, and Alicia Garza created Black Lives Matter and describe it as "an online forum intended to build connections between Black people and our allies to fight anti-Black racism, to spark dialogue among Black people, and to facilitate the types of connections necessary to encourage social action and engagement."

I proudly found myself supporting the movement. Attending events. Leading services. And more . . . I introduced the movement to my congregation. My network. I made connections between Black Lives Matter and the Movement—that is, the Civil Rights Movement—from the sixties when the struggle was centered primarily on voting rights.

And I was all over Black Lives Matter.

And then everything that I knew and understood was turned upside-down on December 15 of that year. I got a text from my daughter Jova, who lived at the time in California in the Bay Area. I had visited her there and loved her home and her work environment but wished that she could live closer. She was about to celebrate her twenty-sixth birthday in New York, and being very close, I was very excited about seeing her.

"Mom, I love you. I love you so much . . ."

Uh-Oh! What did that mean? Every fiber of my being stood at attention.

"Jova, what is going on?"

"I'm sending you the link so you can see what's going on. No matter what happens I'll always love you."

I look at the phone. The phone looks at me.

"Text you later."

"Call me."

"Mom, I can't talk."

"No, Jova, if you don't hang up and call me within the next thirty seconds you won't have a phone to text from." (Yes, I still have her on my family plan . . . Generally a good connector . . .)

"Jova, what on earth is going on?"

"We're about to shut down the Oakland Police."

"What? Are you kidding me?"

"Jova, you are supposed to be coming home for a month next week. Please, *please*, don't come home in a coffin."

"Mom, trust me. I know what I'm doing. We know what we are doing."

"Jova, you might not be as smart as you think you are . . . Please don't do this."

Then the zinger:

"Mom, I am your daughter . . . you taught me to stand for our rights. You taught me to be prepared."

Then the *giga* zinger:

"You taught me the lessons that Grand-Dad taught you. I have to do this. Gotta go . . ."

"You are sure."

"Yes, I'll call you the second it's over, Mom . . ."

"I love you, Jova. Take care . . ."

Many of us don't know what it means to be in the middle of the action because we are on the sidelines. My initial reaction was anger. But by the time she had hung up I had gone over a kaleidoscope of my own activism, particularly as a religious leader.

Back in the day. Charlotte, North Carolina, 1993. I was at a meeting at the Community Church of New York, my home congregation, with all who were heading to General Assembly. I asked about the main event and was told it was the Thomas Jefferson Ball. That was fine.

Fine until the description went on to say: "Come in period dress."

Ouch!!! I recall hearing my twin sister, Janice Marie Johnson, ask, "Well, what am I supposed to wear?"

We tried to get the GA Planning Committee and others to make the theme a "teachable moment" one way or another. Unfortunately, no one listened to us, so we descended on Charlotte knowing where every costume house was! We knew that we had to do *something*. The opportunity presented itself when I went to an African American Ministers meeting and was asked to speak about how people of color felt about the Ball. I said "yes" not realizing that I would need to temper the statement that I had been asked to read—to make it more inclusive of religious leaders of all colors and ethnicities.

Three thousand plus Unitarian Universalists held a collective breath—and could have heard a pin drop. Thirteen people were asked by the moderator to reflect on what had happened and report back to the Plenary session later. We walked off stage, we found a small room where we stood together in a circle, and there we opened up to each other. I was deeply moved by the open and honest sharing of feelings. It was the most profound experience I had ever had. After a little while, we agreed that what had happened was ultimately a good thing. In a democratic faith, we must be able to listen to the pain and anger that is real. We also agreed that no event should be cancelled and that each person must come to their own decision about how to respond and which events to attend.

The ultimate outcome was that though the Thomas Jefferson Ball took place, we were told we could come in period dress, or not. The important point was that everyone knew more than they did before about the reality of racism beyond and within our beloved movement. Thankfully there was no massive walk out, as had happened in the past.

This incident was a defining moment for me. I knew that I needed a place where I could find others who were willing to grapple with the tough stuff. I knew then that this faith was mine and that I would stay no matter how hard it gets.

So, as I returned to Jova and Company shutting down the Oakland Police, I knew that Jova had to do what she felt was right. It's the UU way.

I knew that I needed a place where I could find others who were willing to grapple with the tough stuff. I knew then that this faith was mine and that I would stay no matter how hard it gets.

I want you to know that that evening, while I was waiting with bated breath for Jova's call, I had to attend a conference call. I called the rep from the UUA Board, my friend Michael Sallwasser, so that we could chat before the call.

We spoke for a while until Michael said, "Hope, you don't sound like yourself. What's up?"

There went stoicism. I explained the situation. Michael laughed.

"Michael, what is so funny? I can't believe that you are laughing."

"Hope, my son is there. He's the white photographer. His girlfriend is one of the allies who chained herself to the door. I'm scared too, but our kids are savvy activist UUs and they know what they are doing."

Who knew? Let's take a moment to process this.

It's not enough to have a Black Lives Matter sign if thought is not given to what that really means to you as a congregation, and to you on a personal level. This is a balancing act.

What I learned from Jova was the importance of knowing why I'm doing what I am doing. The importance of doing my homework. The importance of being able to fight for something even in the face of fear.

What does fighting against white supremacy mean to me? What does Black Lives Matter mean to me? Anti-oppression, antiracism, and the celebration of multiculturalism are near and dear to my heart. We liberals have been on the frontlines for a long time.

We are still there. Still here. Struggling. Working together. Figuring out how to deal with our new normal—together! Truth be told, I know of no other place that I'd rather be . . .

As we say at home in Jamaica, "*One love!*"

Jova's Response

A year later, I would be lying if I said that day and the days that followed weren't some of the scariest times of my life. But as my mother said, I was determined to follow my faith and do what I thought was right. In Oakland, I had been involved in direct actions as a means to call attention to the many Black lives that have been killed at the hands of police and various other forms of state-sanctioned violence. I grew up in the church; this church specifically is where I was dedicated and bridged into adulthood, where I learned that the seven Principles are the guiding threads of this thing we call my life. Where I made life-long friends and cultivated my understanding of what it means to be in community—through the good times and the tough ones. As a youth, I started doing UU work beyond the church and was heavily involved in UU organizing on a national level. I was a part of the network of young Unitarian Universalists of color and white allies leading the call to help others develop leadership and social justice-based skills. And now as an adult, having moved from New York, to Massachusetts, to California, and now to Detroit, I find myself without a spiritual home.

Home, as I have been taught, is wherever you make it. But for me as a Black Unitarian Universalist, home is a community that I need to have as a physical space for me to be held and affirmed as I delve deeper into adulthood. And as an adult, I am trying to find the forgiveness in my heart that will allow me to forgive a faith that sometimes does not practice what it preaches. Sometimes we do not treasure the values we say we hold dear when it comes to being actively invested in the search for truth and meaning.

In June of 2005 I was in Fort Worth, Texas, helping to facilitate a youth of color conference prior to General Assembly. During the conference, there were several events that occurred in which staff and congregants of the church were less than welcoming, telling us to shower with a hose, and police were called numerous times because of "suspicious" activity, which was just us sitting outside of the church. The list goes on. Even though faith leaders had apologized to us, little to no follow up occurred—with the exception of defunding programs that helped the conference to happen in the first place.

After returning home, I still believed that things would change, that UU spaces could be a safe place for me. Now, nine years later, I still don't feel safe in most UU spaces. I am no longer able to count how many racist microaggressions my family and I have endured in UU spaces, including church, over the years. It has made me question whether or not I actually have a spiritual home to which I belong. In spite of that, I have always strongly identified as UU. And I am deeply called to seek justice because of my UU faith. So needless to say, there has been some internal conflict. I am UU, but I've been deeply hurt by racist experiences in spaces that I was taught, while growing up, were supposed to be safe for me. I want to be able to go to church, gatherings, and conferences where I can be and feel safe. I want to be able to worship. I want to be able to find a congregation where I am accepted as I am. And although some change has happened since Fort Worth, it still doesn't feel like enough. Whenever I attempt to return, I always leave wondering how folks are really living the seven Principles in their daily lives beyond halls of worship. I know it's hard work; it's work that almost guarantees that someone will mess up, even me. Half the time, I can't remember all of the Principles, but in times where I need grounding and comfort, somehow they always return to me, as though offering me homecoming and relief. I am safe within the seven Principles and I long to be safe at church.

I feel like Unitarian Universalists, particularly white Unitarian Universalists, have a long way to go. I do not need them to feel guilt or shame. I know it's confusing to come to terms with white privilege. And while I do think it's important to turn to Black and people of color in organizing spaces, it is time for white people who are aware of racism to teach, organize, and work with other white people to create change. The Oakland action was a success because white people and Asian allies put their bodies on the line, using their bodies to protect our Black bodies because privilege means that they wouldn't spend more than a few hours in jail if arrested at all. I urge white and other non-Black Unitarian Universalists to help each other become politically educated and then take action in their homes, families, and schools to teach others. I urge folks to volunteer, donate, and spend money in Black-owned/led organizations and businesses. I urge them to follow their faith and truly become active allies, not just bystanders.

It is going to take all of us to create a better world, one that is just and fair. One where Black lives truly matter, so that all lives can begin to matter, because all human life certainly does matter. I want to come back to church and feel safe and welcomed. I want to return to my faith community. And when we change our lives and commit ourselves to justice in an active way, I am sure I will truly be able to return to church and find my spiritual home once again.

Homecoming

REV. JANET BOYKIN JOHNSON
PRELIMINARY FELLOWSHIP 2002, DIED 2015

The date of this sermon and where it was delivered are unknown.

Being here with you this morning, after so long, I am reminded of these words from "Little Gidding" by T.S. Elliot: "The end of all our exploring will be to arrive where we started and to know the place for the first time."

This church is where my love affair with Unitarian Universalism started. When I was about ten years old, I had a close friend who went to a Catholic school. She was required to attend Mass every week, and she would often take me along. The priest spoke in Latin, but everyone seemed to know when to stand, when to kneel, and when to respond. The candles and stained glass pictures of the Madonna and Child produced a rarified atmosphere. I thought that the long strings of colored beads with crosses hanging on them were beautiful and wished that I could be part of this fascinating secret society. I begged my parents to let me go to Catholic school. They adamantly objected. Not only did they think Catholic theology was a bunch of mumbo jumbo, as my father put it, but "why pay money to learn mumbo jumbo?" At that young age, I had no idea what my parents were talking about, and not being allowed to attend Catholic School was one of the biggest disappointments of my young life.

So how did a girl like me end up in a place like this? When I first moved to Chicago to work on my social work degree at the University of Chicago, I met a social work supervisor who was working at the university hospital. Her name was Selina Reed. At the time, she had a teen-aged son named Mark. I told Lee, as she was called by her friends, that I had young children and was looking for a Sunday school for them.

Growing up, my family didn't attend church on a regular basis. Sunday was truly a day of rest in my childhood home. We slept late, read the *New York Times,* and ate big dinners. I decided that I didn't want my children to grow up without a religious education. Lee told me that her church was exactly what I was looking for. My initial intention was to drop the children off, go back home and do a little housework, and then return later to pick them up.

I even thought about taking a little nap in the back of the sanctuary during the service while the children were in church school. Well neither of those things happened. The minister here at the time was Jack Mendelsohn, and after I heard him speak, everything changed. I began attending regularly and became active in the church. I was so impressed by the thoughtful sermons, the church's commitment to inclusiveness, and this church community's concern with religious and ethical issues that I got hooked.

My parents came to visit me during the Christmas holidays in 1975, and I brought them to church with me on Christmas Eve. When it was time for the offering, I put some cash in the collection plate and my father asked me where my church envelopes were. I told him I didn't have any. He told me I wouldn't get credit for the money I placed in the collection plate without envelopes. After that conversation, I officially signed the book on December 26, 1976. Well, even after I joined the church, I didn't get any envelopes, but I became part of a religious community that nurtured and sustained me for more than twenty years.

I felt theologically free to sort out the meaning of life and the nature of the divine for myself while being part of a community of other seekers. Even though I didn't know it at the time, I was entering into a relationship with Unitarian Universalism that would eventually lead me to the ministry.

Lee's son Mark entered the ministry before I did. I remember that Lee was delighted when he did. She died many years ago, and I don't think she lived long enough to see Mark's book, *Black Pioneers in a White Denomination*, become one of the books suggested as required reading for those wishing to enter the UU ministry. I sometimes wonder what she would think about me joining the ranks of the UU ministry knowing that it was her invitation to this church that led me on this path. I tend to feel that she would be delighted by both of these things.

This church sponsored me during my time at Starr King School for the Ministry, provided me with financial support, and ordained me, and I will always think of it as my home church.

There are several ministers who have inspired me along the way, but I only have time to talk briefly about three: The first is Jack Mendelsohn. As I told you before, he was the minister of this church when I joined. I understand he was scheduled to speak here this year but was unable to make the trip. So I'm going to read a passage he wrote:

> A Unitarian Universalist minister is a person never completely satisfied or satisfiable, never completely adjusted or adjustable—a person who walks in two worlds: one of things as they are, the other of things as they ought to be—and loves them both.
>
> Ministers are persons with pincushion souls and elastic hearts, who sit with the happy and the sad in a chaotic pattern of laugh, cry, laugh, cry—and know deep down that the first time their laughter is false or their tears are make-believe, their days as real ministers are over.

Ministers are people with dreams they can never wholly share, partly because they have some doubts about them, and partly because they are unable to explain adequately what it is they think they see and understand.

A minister is a person who continually runs out of time, out of wisdom, out of courage, and out of money; a person whose tasks involve great responsibility and little power, who must learn to accept people where they are and go from there; a person who must never try to exercise influence that has not been earned.

The minister who is worthy knows all this and is still thankful every day of life for the privilege of being—a minister.

The future of the liberal church is almost totally dependent on these two factors: great congregations (whether large or small) and effective, dedicated ministers. The strangest feature of their relationship is that they create one another.[29]

I feel that Jack's words are as relevant today as they were when he wrote them.

After I graduated from Starr King, I worked for four years as a community minister affiliated with the Unitarian Universalist church in Walnut Creek, California. I worked with patients undergoing chemotherapy and was the ministerial presence on the pastoral care committee.

The church that I am currently serving as a parish minister is located in a rural community in central New York. They first met as a Universalist congregation in 1813, and their historic building was completed in 1837. Our building reminds me of a larger Hull Chapel because the ceilings are very similar. Ralph Waldo Emerson, Frederick Douglass, Elizabeth Cady Stanton, and many other notable abolitionists

---

29 Jack Mendelsohn, "Who Is a Unitarian Universalist Minister?" in *Awakened from the Forest: Meditations on Ministry*, edited by Gary E. Smith (Skinner House Books, 1995).

and suffragists spoke there over the years. Martin Luther King Jr. held a meeting in our social hall in 1956 while he was attending the Universalist Convention that year. I feel honored to share the same pulpit and church space that these notable people were in.

This brings me to the second minister I want to talk about today, Rev. Kenneth Patton. I never met him, and what I know about him comes from studying UU history. He was a confirmed Humanist identified as one of the major poets and a prophet of contemporary liberal religion. He was not a perfect man. He was outspoken and provocative. His preaching offended many, including his more conservative colleagues. He was verbally combative with other ministers and religious leaders. His ministerial manner drove parishioners away. His single-mindedness led him to ignore others' concerns and to respond with irritation to their needs. Often he refused to compromise or even listen to other points of view. Nevertheless, I am impressed with what he offered our religious movement. Here's why: He served both Unitarian and Universalist churches before the merger. He wrote extensively about worship and the function of religion. But I think the most important work he did was when he became minister of the Charles Street Meeting House in 1949. The Universalist Church of America had been in decline for much of the twentieth century and needed to find an infusion of strength. The Charles Street Meeting House was an experimental church in Boston created by the Massachusetts Universalist Convention to revitalize Universalism and to reinstate a Universalist presence in Boston. Since the Universalist traditional message, that a loving God would not condemn anyone to hell, had been accepted by other denominations, Universalists needed a new focus and a wider scope.

Patton, during his ministry, redefined the meaning of the word *Universalism* by bringing the arts of all religions and cultures into "a religion for one world." Many of the hymns and readings used in the Meeting House services became part of the 1964 hymnal, *Hymns for the Celebration of Life.* Old hymn tunes came to new life with his words. The symbols of most of the world religions that decorated the meeting house now decorate the fireside room at Starr King. Patton wrote,

> All life flows into a great common life, if we will only open ourselves
> to our companions. We listen to the secret voices of poetry and know
> that all people men share our yearning. All are lonely as we are lonely,
> and all need the sure presence of those who love and are loved.[30]

Reverend Peter Morales, newly elected president of the UUA, wants Unitarian Universalism to be a religion for our time. I think that Patton was ahead of his time, and I also think that in order to be a religion for our time we need to recover the genius of his type of Universalism—that is, the idea of a religious human family. What Patton meant was an acceptance of world religions and drawing from them for our worship services. I think that we have learned that our religious experience is enhanced if we open our minds and hearts to teachings from the world religions. In addition, we recognize that we simply cannot afford to be dismissive of anyone's religion, for our own sake and for the sake of world peace. I think that from the past to the present, Unitarian Universalists, regardless of their individual beliefs about God, the Bible, Jesus, the earth, death, prayer, and ritual, expect to have their minds and their spirits fed in church. We are a religious movement that fully appreciates the contributions and benefits of reason and critical thinking. At the same time, we know that there is much in life that is mysterious and awe inspiring that can only be experienced and not dissected and analyzed.

---

30 The source of this version of "Let Us Worship" by Kenneth L. Patton is unknown, although it is quoted as "Responsive Reading 372" in "Full Text of 1974 Orders of Service" (Unitarian Church of Greensboro, NC) at Internet Archive, https://archive.org. This version appears to be adapted from an original that used "men" instead of "people" and "all men" instead of "all."

In worship we draw on the magic that happens all around us and the mind's ability to reason things out.

Do we share our faith with others? We don't and I would suggest that one of the reasons our churches don't grow is because we don't evangelize (if you will). Just for the record, there is a difference between proselytizing and evangelizing. People who proselytize want to convert others to their religion. People who evangelize simply spread the good news. That is what Selina Reed did when she heard me say I was looking for a church school.

Some of us don't evangelize because we don't know much about our faith beyond the idea that it's okay to believe anything you want. This sounds simple enough, but it ends up being very difficult to explain in forty-five seconds or less to someone who asks what UUs believe.

I think the main reason we don't say much about our faith is that we don't want to be perceived as religious by others. We are afraid people will make assumptions about us based on their notions of what a religious person is. On the flip side, we fear rejection by others once they do know more about our faith.

Each and every one of us needs to reach out to friends and family and precisely articulate what we stand for. If we do so, our movement might grow instead of declining.

Finally, my third ministerial role model is theologian and modern mystic Reverend Howard Thurman. My mother told me about him when I was a young girl. He was a professor of religion and philosophy and a religious advisor at Spelman College when she was a student there. He often preached in the college chapel and made a profound impression on her. When I was older, she introduced me to Thurman's books, and I

Each and every one of us needs to reach out to friends and family and precisely articulate what we stand for. If we do so, our movement might grow instead of declining.

was as moved by his writings as she had been. He is considered one of the most creative religious minds.

Thurman was not a Martin Luther King or a Jesse Jackson. He saw his role as that of teacher and enabler. People like King, Jackson, and other revolutionary Black preachers went to Thurman for renewal and council. In quiet moments before a civil rights march, King used to read from Thurman's book, *Jesus and the Disinherited*. Only through love, Thurman writes, can people surmount what divides them. This love must be rooted in the "deep river" of faith: It may twist and turn, fall back on itself, and start again, stumble over an infinite series of hindering rocks, but at last the river must answer the call to the sea. He believed that if one established a spiritual harmony with oneself, with God, with nature, and with others, the harmony itself would translate into justice. He developed a universal spirit and was always searching for what was common in people and in the religious experience. He was another person who was ahead of his time and whose philosophy is probably still far ahead of many.

According to several sources, Howard Thurman would always begin his sermons by reading a portion of the 139th Psalm, and I would like to end this talk with that passage:

> O, Lord, where can I go from your Spirit?
> Where can I flee from your presence? If I go up to the heavens,
> you are there; If I make my bed in the depths, you are there. If I rise on
> the wings of the dawn, if I settle on the far side of the sea,
> even there your hand will guide me, your right hand
> will hold me fast.[31]

---

31 *Editor's note:* Translation unknown.

Ubuntu:
I Am Because We Are

REV. DR. REBEKAH A. SAVAGE
PRELIMINARY FELLOWSHIP 2002,
FULL FELLOWSHIP 2012

By all accounts, I should not be here. I am a Black-identified, multi-racial Unitarian Universalist minister in final fellowship. I was raised UU in a predominantly white congregation in a predominantly white denomination. I was raised in an area where kids and families didn't look like mine, and my role models and mentors didn't either. When so many before me were not able to stay in our midst, I am mindful that I should not be here. I am here because of so many good souls and open-hearted encouragements that put me in places and with people that made me who I am today. And I am filled with gratitude for those who went before me and made my small existence possible. I am because We Are. We are generations of BIPOC Unitarian Universalists, known and unknown, who have made our movement in this great turning possible.

I am thankful for my forebears, like Rev. Marjorie Bowens-Wheatley. After I graduated from seminary in 1999, I was living in Florida and found myself rather adrift spiritually and lacking commu-nity. I felt uprooted and unsure of where my professional career would take me. I recall clearly the day that Rev. Marjorie invited me to her home for tea. I was young and still very much in formation and I felt as if I had been summoned by a Great Teacher. I remember we sat together, side by side on spacious chairs, and Rev. Marjorie sought to just know me. She saw me and I felt encouragement simply with her gracious hospitality. I remember she said to me, "You're important. We need you. Don't forget that."

I am thankful for community. Many people may not realize the power of community. The power of being with people and in spaces that are like islands of refuge in the midst of feeling isolated and marginalized. At General Assembly, I remember feeling awestruck by walking into the DRUUMM (Diverse Revolutionary UU Multicultural Ministries) reception before the Ware Lecture, presented by President Barack Obama's inaugural poet Richard Blanco. I couldn't make it past the door for a good few minutes. Awe froze me in place. I stood in the doorway and just looked around the room, taking in the sight before me. Black UUs. Brown UUs. Asian UUs. Latinx UUs. Multiracial UUs. Indigenous UUs. Our BIPOC UU Elders. Our BIPOC UU young adults, youth, and children. Couples and families gathered around tables with smiles and warmth and heart that made the room feel like a huge family reunion where many of us were meeting for the first time. It didn't matter. We were home to each other in that moment. The image of that room, alive and pulsing with our living history, comes to me when I am bewildered, confused, and saddened by a world that can feel so hard at times. The power of community gives me strength.

I am thankful for the challenge of dismantling white supremacy culture. It's been hard work, soul work, that requires that I humble myself to acknowledge my own complicity in a system that is destroying lives and communities and even hastening the destruction of our planet. I can only call upon others to take on this dismantling, this great turning, by doing the work within myself first. And the work requires listening, slowing down conversations, and centering care first. I've learned this the hard way, when rapid-fire agendas and the urge for task completion fracture relationships and strain good will. I have thus found a higher tolerance for spaciousness, for letting energy find rest in our gentle keeping so that there is room to continue on. Sometimes that means not making hasty decisions. Sometimes that means going for a walk instead of reacting in the moment. Sometimes that means calling my people and asking for their care and witness. Sometimes that means weeping for all that we have lost and all that we are losing due to fear, antipathy, and knee-jerk defensiveness. Sometimes that means dancing with Spirit and welcoming the messiness of complicated lives in transformation. I am thankful for it all.

I am thankful for my calling as a UU minister. I lived into my calling over time and it hasn't been an easy road to navigate. I have wrestled with self-doubt and feelings of inadequacy, giving too much attention to insidious voices, both real and imagined, that lobbed accusations at me that I was a failure, not good enough, unworthy. As a Black-identified, multiracial UU minister, two core virtues serve as foundations of my life and calling: service and sacrifice. Service as a virtue is a form of sacred stewardship, as I have been bestowed unearned blessings that are now mine to care for and share, only because of those who went before me, for the good of others. My Ancestors survived long enough to make their mark on this world by bringing progeny into it, and I am mindful of how my service honors them. The blessings I have been given are only mine to give away. One of the best aspects of being a military chaplain when I served was to be surrounded by the expectations of being active. I often joked that physical training was my love language: running, lifting weights, yoga, martial arts, and long, meditative hikes with a heavy rucksack. As a chaplain, it was an easy way to connect with other service members. They often were highly amused and motivated to see their chaplain rock physical fitness standards, and I'd simply respond, "I'm blessed to be a blessing." My strength, endurance, and prowess are not mine; they are gifts to be used fully in service of something greater than myself, to encourage others around me and make it known what is possible for them to do. So a marathon carrying a fifty-pound pack? Too easy. I'll pray and sing to myself for the seven hours it takes to complete it.

The idea of sacrifice as a virtue is a recognition that I choose again and again to pay attention to the margins, attentive to Spirit. Transformation and every justice movement begin on the margins, with those most impacted and disenfranchised. While I may not be able to quiet the self-doubt, I can go back to spiritual practices that connect me with service and sacrifice, in honor of those who have gone before me to make my ministry and my very life possible.

By all accounts, I should not be here. It is my prayer that no one ever again finds truth in this statement. It is my prayerful intention to be a part of what makes that possible. I am because We Are.

I love what I do. And I love who I am so much that I want her to be more. The future is limitless for all of us. I simply want to be a presence who encourages others to be their most present selves. If someone had told me that I would be who I am doing what I do, I would never have believed them. That is the beauty of life: its limitless possibilities.

> *I love what I do. And I love who I am so much that I want her to be more.*

Being a priestess, a woman of the cloth, an agent of healing in this world, is a solitary path. It sets us apart. It can be a very lonely place. Women of color have a lot of demands placed on us because our families and communities are, more often than not, economically challenged. Moreover, the responsibility of caring for families is disproportionately placed on women, especially women of African descent.

The biggest hurdle that I have had to face are the social exigencies, the expectations to be "good." Just plain good—a good wife, a good mother, a good girl, a good chaplain—when sometimes life around us is not quite that good. Sometimes it's downright shitty. The artist in me would call those times "material" or grist for the mill. "There is no bad experience," I'd say, because it can all go into feeding the creative voice.

Ministers are expected, realistically or not, to have moved beyond life's challenges, to have "arrived" or become perfected in some sense. Yet how do you hold up the world when yours is fractured, frail, and crumbling? It helps to have a strong support system that is willing to hold you through the difficult days. There will inevitably be some. We Unitarian Universalist military chaplains are few, and we are strong. Our strength comes from the bonds that we have forged, due in vast part to our endorser, Rev. Sarah Lammert, and the multitude of souls who support our ministry from behind the scenes. We are blessed to have an annual pilgrimage in which we come together. These moments have proven invaluable to my ministry. To have a center to return to in the midst of all of the changes that one goes through as a military chaplain is invaluable. I have grown through these reunions and such growth has added enormously to my ministry.

Journeys That Lead to the Heart

REV. DR. AZANDE SASA

PRELIMINARY FELLOWSHIP 2002,
FULL FELLOWSHIP 2015

In every life, there are significant moments that inform our understanding of what it means to walk in this world as a spiritual being. Often, these events occur in our formative years though we may not make sense of them at the time.

My conception of what it means to be a spiritual being has been inspired by a few pivotal events that have dotted my life landscape. Early on, I learned that religion can be an unsafe place. You are either in or out.

First, there was Joy. She was my friend. In the summer, we would play every day from sunup to sundown. If I was not at her house, she was at my house. She was my friend. One day, I could no longer play with her. "I am a Jehovah's Witness," she said.

"What's that?" I replied. I had no idea what it meant. I only knew that my best friend was gone. While she still lived across the alley from me, I could no longer play with her. We no longer enjoyed long summer days.

Then there was a family who lived next door to my grandmother. I went to play with their daughter, who was also in the first grade. I knocked on the door.

"Is Judie home?"

"No."

"But I just saw her."

"Go away," said Mr. Ward, her father.

"Please, can she come out?"

"No."

"But why?"

"Go away, you devil!"

Mr. Ward hit me with the back of his hand. I flew down the stairs and ran away crying. The busted lip eventually healed, but I will never forget those words. These experiences have indelibly shaped my faith journey, but they will never limit it.

I give credit to these tough life lessons. I would not be a Unitarian Universalist clergy member today if it were not for this series of seeming mishaps, misfires, and plenty of grace-full people who guided my steps. Every experience has fed into where and who I am today. There are no accidents. No mistakes. There were so many blessings that turned out to be misfortunes and so many misfortunes that led me back home. Ministry is part and parcel of my predicament of being *neti neti*—neither this nor that, to borrow from the Sanskrit term. It was not just pivotal events around religion but identity that spurred my greater search for truth and meaning, which continues even to the present.

"God doesn't make mistakes." That was my mother's mantra when I would get into fits of not wanting to be me. As a South-Sudanese-African American or, what at times felt like a Sudo-American, I grew up with a visibly African appearance in a midwestern town that was not known for its cultural diversity. As a result, I was taunted endlessly for having skin that was too dark and hair that was too nappy. There are times when just being present is enough to ignite a fire.

There are times when just being present is enough to ignite a fire.

When I was in the first grade, there was a family who lived on the corner that had six children—one for each grade. After school, when we got off of the bus, they took turns beating me until one of the neighbors would come out and break it up. My appearance was too "African" for their liking. What was so disorienting was the fact that they were Black as well. I grew up feeling that the threat to my existence came not from people who did not look like me but from those who did.

I became comfortable with the "other" because they didn't care what my complexion or my hair looked like. Through my experiences of being on the receiving end of such violence, I found it futile to fight back so I escaped through books. At age fourteen, I had the opportunity to attend an elite college preparatory school. There I became the "scholarship kid" and the only Black student in my class. As "the one," I was comfortably uncomfortable. No one teased me about my hair. In fact, no one bothered me at all. I was present but absent. Being "the one" is lonely but necessary at times. In the absence of others like you, just being is a powerful statement.

In my senior year, we read a range of mind-expanding literature, including *The Autobiography of Malcom X.* These readings opened my world. From Malcolm, I learned that it was systemic racism that had created a pervasive self-hate among African-descended people that manifested across playgrounds and bus stops across the country. Most importantly, I learned that Black could be beautiful. I exulted and ran to the source of my persecution—my Africanity. I embraced my Africanness because that was the thing that was most hated by the world and so needed my love and my nurturance. Now I neither run from who I am nor toward the exterior clothing that I have inherited in this life. I just am. We just are. We are, all of us, beautiful. God doesn't make mistakes.

Based on my past, I believe every experience is fruitful. I have learned that I never want to judge someone based on the way they look, the color of their skin, their gender identity and expression, or their belief system or lack thereof. This is a continuous faith practice toward which I strive. When I discovered Unitarian Universalism, it opened a door to my soul. To be around people who are like you is not as important as being around people of like mind, like heart, like sentiment, but different enough to challenge you to be your better self.

Hate is debilitating and exhausting. It is more life affirming to be *for* something than to be perpetually *against* everything. These are the experiences that have formed my faith journey. This is the faith journey that informs who I am.

My first steps as a Unitarian Universalist are inextricably linked to my predicament as a seeker on a path of self-awareness. What I discovered was more than I ever imagined. I was raised Lutheran, and I found myself, through the years, needing to find a faith that allowed me to more fully embrace the totality of who I am and my direct experiences with the Divine.

My faith journey has been, in part, inherited. But what does it mean to inherit a faith? Is it evident in the platelets of our blood, the curvature of our DNA? What is the genealogy that leads to our belief? Or disbelief?

I have always felt the presence of my Ancestors. My continuous connection with them has elicited a deeper meaning to life. These interfaces have proven more formative than anything that anyone of *any* authority, or none at all, could tell me—or any experience that I could read about in a book. I believe what Yeshua said: "Whoever believes in me will do the works I have been doing, and they will do even greater things than these" (John 14:12). I longed for the "religion *of* Christ not the religion *about* Christ." I sought a faith in which no one was left out of the sanctuary. I desperately needed a belief system that would push me to explore higher truths and meaning.

I am convinced that my mother was a Unitarian Universalist at heart. She lived her faith without wearing her religion on her sleeve. I recall conversations about her visit to a Baha'i church when she was new on her journey. As a youth, she questioned why an all-Black church would have a picture of a blond-haired, blue-eyed Jesus on the wall and why an unmarried pregnant girl had to stand in front of the congregation and beg for forgiveness. The most important faith lesson from my mother was that to love others means to accept them for who they are without attempting to transform them into who we believe they should be.

In college, I majored in comparative and regional studies of Africa and Latin America at Georgetown University's School of Foreign Service. I was curious about how the intersection of ethnicity, culture, and historical experiences of colonialism and slavery shaped religion. In my personal family history, I often wondered why my grandmother would never attend funerals or weddings. And why my African Anglican father never stepped foot in a church while he was in America. It is the composite of these lived and learned experiences, conveyed through shared story, that pours into the making of who we are. Our unfolding faith journeys are often winding spirals that lead to the heart.

Some of the most formative faith experiences are those that occur repeatedly throughout our lives. I have been blessed to have had several brushes with death. I say blessed because each occasion gave me an intimate awareness of the Divine. I would not change a thing. In those moments, on the precipice between life and death, I realized there is no finality, at least not to my existence. These experiences have left me not with a belief, but with a knowingness that undergirds a determination to love everyone. Our superficial differences are just that, superficial. There is something much deeper.

These experiences of near-death have profoundly affected my ability to embrace all and deeply informed my ministry. Be willing to love and embrace; never be too sure in your unknowing that you are unwilling to listen to another.

One day, I saw Mr. Ward as an adult. I questioned what welled within me. When my sentiments caught up with what my eyes beheld, I realized that he was old, frail, and harmless. Was my faith large enough to embrace this man? This soul? To forgive? To see him not for what he did, but for who he was? A child of God. In hindsight, I understand that these experiences, however painful at the time, allowed me to simultaneously be at home no place and every place—to be able to gather with those from radically different backgrounds and still connect. This has been immensely helpful for work as a chaplain. These heart-expanding experiences open our eyes to who we truly are. It is the weaving together of these experiences into a cloak of understanding that brings us to peace.

I have also been blessed to have teachers early in life, mentors who inspired me to be who I am, a truly spiritual being. That is what we are here to be. If that is all that I do, I have lived a good life.

I have always felt called to do creative and spiritual work. I manifested my call to the arts early on as an actor. In college, I played a pastor named Margaret Alexander in *The Amen Corner*. Thanks to James Baldwin, I realized that I felt very much at home in the pulpit—even if it was on stage. James Baldwin's play was a seedling event in my life.

My first big "break" came when I got a Levi's Jeans commercial. I made a lot of money doing nothing. While it was initially rewarding, it was at the same time unsettling. It didn't seem right that someone could do so little and make so much money. It rubbed against my sense of justice. In hindsight, I must have been out of my mind. I wish I could make enough money in one day to live off for an entire year. But at that time, my idealism was very strong.

My creative pursuits grew to encompass creative writing, which landed me at Brown University, where I achieved my Master of Fine Arts degree in playwriting under the tutelage of giants such as the late Aisha Rahman and Paula Vogel. In that two-year program, I wrote and wrote and wrote my heart out. It was as if I emptied out my soul. In fact, I did. And at the end of those two years, once again, I felt the stir of the call. The voice within said, "I want to do something to serve God and humanity." My call led me to Harvard Divinity School, where I completed my Master of Divinity degree.

Quite frankly, I was young when I graduated from divinity school and went off to begin my ministry. I had the fortune, which I interpreted as a misfortune at the time, of being laid off from my first full-time ministerial position. This setback provided an opportunity for me to return to school to obtain my Ph.D. in sociocultural anthropology. I felt that I needed a little more seasoning for ministry, and this program would allow me the opportunity to grow. But eight years into the program, having completed all but my dissertation, I was weary and once again felt the stir of the call.

One day while driving, I reflected upon my journey. I had come to a life crossroad. I was pondering whether or not to resume my ministry after such a long hiatus. It could have gone either way. And words I have rarely uttered came to the surface, "God, if it is meant for me to be a chaplain, please give me a sign." Just then, I noticed a flashing triangle with an exclamation mark in the middle. I had asked the Divine Source for a sign and there it was, but I didn't realize it because I was so distracted *by* the sign that I didn't *see* the sign. I looked to my left. There was an AAMCO. I turned. I asked the attendant, "Is there something wrong with my car?"

"Well, let's take a look at it," he said. He saw the flashing sign and said, "That just means that your air pressure's low. Here, let me show you how to check all your tires." He walked around to every single tire, showed me how to check the pressure, and added air when they were low. At the last tire, he handed me the instrument and said, "Here, I want you to do the last one, so I know that you know how to do it." I checked it and added air.

"Thank you so much!" I said, "What can I give you for your trouble?"

"It was no trouble at all," he said. "All I want you to do is spread the word."

At that moment, I remembered the question that spurred these events. I remembered that I had just asked for a sign, and I received one.

I still have the tire pressure checker that he gave me because that is a tangible reminder of how the holy intervenes in our lives to reassure us of who we are and what we are here to do. Every time that I get to doubting, wavering and wondering, who am I? Why am I here? Am I making any difference? I remember that I am called to do this and so I bring my best self to this sacred and joyful task. The funny thing is, I'm sure he did not know what he did. He may not have even been a real person. He may have even been an angel in disguise. In fact, I am sure he was, in the truest sense of the word, a messenger.

The Path to Ministry

REV. ADDAE AMA KRABA
PRELIMINARY FELLOWSHIP 2004

Before receiving a call to ministry, I had never heard of Unitarian Universalism. I had been a faithful Catholic before I left the church. The call came in a spiritual metaphysical form that surprised me. However, after answering yes, I was at a loss as to where I would find the next step in my spiritual journey. But answers to questions sometimes come from the most unlikely sources. I have four sons, and one is well versed in world religions. He suggested that I should consider going to the Unitarian Universalists because in his opinion, they were a lot like me.

One Sunday morning instead of going to the service at the Unity church that I was currently attending, I got off the bus on the corner of Geary and Franklin Streets and walked through the doors of First Unitarian Society of San Francisco. It was one of those Sundays when tables are set up by the various committees in the congregation providing pamphlets with information on the functions of each one. I was in such awe of the plethora of options to serve that I was sold before ever attending a worship service.

I not only found a new way to worship; I also found a congregation that believed in good and the importance of giving back to community, and that has always been important to me. The congregation had co-ministers, one male and one female. I met with both, informing them of my intention to attend seminary. I soon signed the membership book, and the congregation became my sponsoring church for my enrollment as a student in Starr King School for the Ministry; the female minister became my mentor.

During my years in seminary, I was surrounded by both students and educators who were caring and supportive, and as I learned about Unitarian Universalism, I also experienced tremendous spiritual growth. By the time I graduated, I had gained so much self-knowledge that I felt that the time and money invested was more than worth it, even if I never worked a day in ministry.

Because Community Church of New York had a history of breaking color barriers by making a concerted effort to invite and support African American membership, it was the only congregation that I applied to serve as intern. My internship was both challenging and wonderful. Challenging because I was thrown into the deep end with far more pulpit time than I felt prepared for, but wonderful because I was nurtured by and felt the love and support of the congregation, particularly the African American church ladies. I was able to develop a preaching style that is uniquely mine.

I was apprehensive about seeking a settlement immediately after graduation, so I decided to apply for a chaplain residency, which helped me along the path of spiritual growth. When I finally decided to go into search for a congregation to settle in, it was more because I wanted to take a leap into the unknown and challenge myself as a congregational leader than because of a desire to lead a congregation. I was the first minister of color in the congregation's 150-year history. It didn't take very long to discover how many challenges and roadblocks occur when ministers of color attempt to serve all-white congregations. Many members view hiring a minister of color as the endpoint of any expanded learning about white privilege and systemic racism. I have also found that many of the men struggle to accept Black women in the leadership and react in a passive aggressive way to decisions made. During the five years that I served, I found that the level of disrespect and thoughtlessness was boundless.

I recall a Sunday morning when a male member of my congregation bypassed the church hall to tape a flyer announcing his daughter's concert on the prayer rail in the sanctuary as people were gathering for Sunday service.

One instance of blatant disrespect came from an invited guest speaker. He was a local artist who was to share the source of his inspiration. There was to be no filming in the sanctuary and Q&A would be conducted during coffee hour. He agreed to the conditions, but then proceeded to shorten his information and take the handheld mic and call for Q&A. I was unfettered by his assumption that I wouldn't interrupt him, so I walked over and asked that his Q&A wait until after we concluded worship. This was one of those occasions when my congregation supported me in claiming authority as their leader.

Many members view hiring a minister of color as the endpoint of any expanded learning about white privilege and systemic racism.

Some incidents of disrespect were not blatantly racist, but thoughtless and indicative of inability to relate to cultures unlike one's own. For instance, in a group discussion in which I was present, somehow the discussion turned to citizenship and one woman said, "All of our ancestors came to this country for a better life." I was flabbergasted by the thoughtlessness of that one individual, but even more so that everyone else was unfazed by the statement. The conversation continued as if nothing untoward had occurred.

After my trip to Africa in 2008, I wrote a sermon about my cultural pilgrimage and delivered it to various congregations across the country and several local civic groups. In the sermon, I talk about the many tears I shed while tracing the footsteps of my ancestors, particularly after standing in the dungeons at Cape Coast Castle and again while looking at the vast ocean through the window of no return. The sermon was well received each time I shared my experience from the pulpit, and it became an entry point for discussions about slavery. To my dismay, the only exception came after sharing the experience from the pulpit of the congregation that I was serving at the time. When the service ended and the congregation filed past me into the parish hall, most of them met me with awkward silence and avoided eye contact. The only feedback that I received came sometime later when a man in the congregation asked, "What was so hard about your trip to Africa?" I responded that it was a painful reminder of how much suffering my ancestors endured being snatched from their homeland to be enslaved on the other side of the world. But in those moments, I still wonder how a former public school educator and fifth-generation Universalist could ask such a question.

On more than one occasion, I have been greeted by people at district gatherings and at General Assembly mistaking me for some other colleague of color. I find that disturbing because it implies that collectively we are viewed as persons of color rather than individuals with unique attributes and personalities. Meanwhile, some of these same people complain about and question the lack of racial diversity in our congregations. The irony of being a minister of color in this denomination is that finding a home under the umbrella of Unitarian Universalism is the result of seeking a place that affirms without prejudice, and yet even here we find some of the same prejudices within our midst. Ministry is challenging in and of itself, and this added burden makes it more difficult to serve.

However, with all of the negative sides to serving in our congregations, I have encountered some very caring and loving people who keep me hopeful. These are the individuals who live life guided by our seven Principles. I've had more ups than downs, and the support that I've received makes up for some of the mean-spirited behavior. It's not to say that I'm not annoyed or sometimes angered by some of the negative actions, but into every life some rain must fall.

My professional role as minister is intertwined with my personal self, mind, body, and spirit; my interactions with people in the congregation are the same as with people at the mall or in the supermarket. I truly believe in good, knowing that each of us possesses a spark connecting us to the divine. Therefore, I don't place unrealistic expectations on people because they've been nurtured within a patriarchal society that has deep roots in systemic racism supporting a belief that people of color are inferior or fall short in some way. Ministry has been a series of firsts for me, beginning with the call to settle in a congregation that had never had a person of color serve in that capacity in its 150-year history. That same thing is true in the five other congregations that followed. Sometimes I'm proud that I have been the individual to make inroads; other times, I find the effort exhausting. But there are far more rewards than disappointments.

Rites of passage are rewarding, particularly weddings and baby blessings because there is so much hope and joy in people's lives on these occasions. It's also extremely humbling to be a comfort to people from the wider community who seek us out when mourning the deaths of loved ones. On these occasions, the unchurched turn to us as a last beacon of hope to bring dignity to a final rite. I find this to be such a reaffirmation of my call to serve.

The mantle that ministers wear can be heavy, and the journey can prove to be lonely, mainly because so much is expected of us. I would also venture to say that trust is a primary issue, for both congregants and ministers alike. It takes time to build trust, but sometimes we stay in congregations only long enough to make just a little headway in relationships before we have to part ways.

However, with all of the challenges and roadblocks, I'd say yes again, because knowing that you are fulfilling your destiny because you want to, rather than because you have to, makes a huge difference. The journey becomes an adventure, and every experience is an opportunity to be the best human being that I can be. I made decisions about ministry based on the best that I had to offer at the time; I asked for help from mentors when needed, so that I could act in the best interest of all concerned. My ministry has been rewarding, and I would do it all over again.

In One Moment

REV. CHERYL M. WALKER
PRELIMINARY FELLOWSHIP 2005, FULL FELLOWSHIP 2009

Shortly after the murder of George Floyd by Minneapolis police, I preached a sermon entitled "The Tipping Point." I did not preach it the week immediately after Mr. Floyd was killed because as I told the congregation, "I don't have the words yet. If you were hoping I would help you find comfort in these troubling times, well I have no desire for you or anyone to be comfortable right now." In the week that followed, I found my words.

In my sermon of June 7, 2020, I spoke to the fact that I had been receiving a lot of text messages from random white people saying they loved me, and that as a Black woman in America, I didn't need love texts from white people with unlimited texting. I then gave a list of what I thought Black people needed from white people. Since our services are online due to the COVID-19 pandemic, people often put messages in the chat. As I was preaching, someone wrote, "What should we do?" in the chat. Ironically, or befittingly, it was just before I said, "What I need from white people is to stop asking me what you should do. It's your work; mine is different."

Not a minute later, the same person typed in the chat, "Just to be clear, I am asking you as my minister." And in that one moment, all that I knew about being a Black lesbian woman in ministry in Unitarian Universalism came together. I was invisible as a person; I am a minister. I was invisible as a person; I am a Black lesbian minister. I was invisible as a person; I am a woman. I was invisible as a person; I am Black.

I cannot say I was surprised. I have been a Black lesbian Unitarian Universalist minister for quite a few years, and I have seen and heard almost everything. Not being surprised still did not keep my heart from breaking just a little more when I read those words. I say a little more because in the profession of ministry, your heart gets broken, and being a Black woman in our faith means your heart gets broken a lot. It hurts each and every time. The microaggressions hurt as much as the overt aggressions hurt.

In that one moment, I thought, "Oh my, we still have so much to do. My work here is not done." My work, my calling, is to help our people and our faith live up to the promise that I believed it offered when I came into this faith so many years ago. It was the promise of loving communities of faith that embraced and celebrated all of our differences and recognized the beauty and spark of the holy in each and every person. It is why I came into this faith, why I stay in this faith, why I answered the call to ministry, and why I have hope that one day we shall be who we profess to be. We are not there yet, but the journey is not over.

Coming into the Faith

I was not born into Unitarian Universalism; I came into the faith from the wilderness. While I was raised in a different faith tradition, I had long ago set it aside because it did not fill my needs. There were parts that I loved, but I knew it would not be the place my soul could call home. I studied a lot of religions, and while there were parts of each of them that spoke to my soul, none of them were quite right. So I lived in a spiritual wilderness for a long time.

It wasn't until a good friend of mine introduced me to Unitarian Universalism that I finally found my place. When I entered the sanctuary of the Community Church of New York and saw banners representing different religions, I knew instinctively that I was in the right place.

It was a visual statement of the idea that there are many paths on our spiritual journeys and wisdom from many sources. Those banners said, without words, "We draw upon the full depth and breadth of the human experience." It helped that the minister who preached that morning was the late Rev. Marjorie Bowens-Wheatley, a Black woman.

The Community Church of New York wasn't my first experience in a Unitarian Universalist congregation. The same friend had taken me to the Unitarian Church of Montclair, New Jersey. What these two congregations had in common was the fact that they were both racially diverse. They were both Welcoming Congregations, embracing the LGBTQ community. I believed that all Unitarian Universalist congregations were this way—diverse, open, and welcoming. Yet I was hesitant to become a member. I kept having a nagging suspicion that this was too good to be true. Could it really be true that there was a religion where I was free to explore my spiritual beliefs and be fully accepted and embraced as Black, lesbian, a woman? I had my doubts.

My doubts were confirmed when I went to my first General Assembly. I was shocked by how white things were. White people, white music, white worship, white everything, with a smattering of People of Color who were paraded forward when it was convenient and then "invisibilized" when it was not. Where were the People of Color in leadership? At the time, there were none. There were very few women in leadership, and no openly out queer people in leadership. I heard a lot of talk about diversity and inclusion, but saw very little diversity and inclusion in leadership and in the membership. In that moment I knew who we really were, and when I got back to Community Church, I finally signed the membership book.

I knew the truth of how far we were from who we say we are, or at least say we want to be. And because I knew the truth, I knew the challenge of being in this faith. But I also knew that while this was a faith that was predominantly white, it was also a faith of great promise. It named its own problem, and it said it wanted to do something about it. I knew from my experiences in life that this was a start, because you can't solve a problem you don't think you have. I also knew that it might be especially challenging for white liberal people because white liberal people are still acculturated to be white people first, and too often think they are somehow immune to racist thoughts and actions. But the promise of the faith outweighed the challenges it presented, and I was willing to be part of a faith community that I knew would break my heart, and that I also knew would fill my soul.

> *The promise of the faith outweighed the challenges it presented, and I was willing to be part of a faith community that I knew would break my heart, and that I also knew would fill my soul.*

Surviving the Faith

In my many years of being a Unitarian Universalist, I am often asked by other People of Color, "Why do you stay? Why stay in a faith that professes so much promise and disappoints so many times?"

I have three answers. One: this is my faith home because I have no place else to go. Theologically, this is the only place for my soul. I came into this faith not for community, but for the theology, the openness to explore. Two: every community of people will disappoint you because people are imperfect. The shiny glow you found when you first arrived will lose its patina very quickly. This is true of our communities and any community. Three: you cannot change Unitarian Universalism if you are not a part of it. There is much to be hopeful about in this faith and its communities, but if you are not a part of them, you cannot change them.

Then I give them some pieces of advice. Find your allies and your friends. Find the people—and they are here—who are willing to stay in the struggle with you; those will be your allies. Your allies will be of all races, sexes, genders, ages, orientations, and other permutations of humanity. Then find some friends. People with whom you can just openly be yourself. They are here too. And like allies, they may be of any permutation of humanity. Be a good friend to them, and they will be good friends to you. But you've got to have friends. You cannot survive anything alone.

Keep doing your spiritual work. This is a faith community, not a social club and not a social justice club. If you came here for the faith, do the work of your own faith formation. The beauty and the challenge of Unitarian Universalism is that it will not give you the answers to your faith journey. It is yours to do, and without a solid grounding in your spiritual life, you will not be able to do the work of justice making, of changing Unitarian Universalism, or of just being in UU communities. Keep feeding your spirit.

And then finally, be patient. Evolution is a slow process, but when we evolve, we are forever changed. There is no devolution. It took hundreds of years to create the Unitarian Universalism of today; it will take many more to create the Unitarian Universalism of tomorrow, the one you dream about. Sometimes you'll need some holy impatience, but you must be patient. It is the only way to survive this faith.

The Calling

I was content to just be a member of Community Church for years. I went to services almost every Sunday; I was involved in different committees; I made friends and worked on social justice issues. I took my faith into the rest of my life. It inspired me to work differently. I asked myself in dealing with people how I was exemplifying my Unitarian Universalist values. Did I treat people with dignity and respect? Was I embracing their differences? Was I loving? Even working on Wall

Street, which I did as a vice president in technology for a large brokerage house, I tried to bring my values into my workplace.

One of the things I did was volunteer at a homeless shelter run by Community Church. It made me reassess my life. I realized that I was complicit in making people homeless, because I was working in a system in which people who had more than enough kept thinking it wasn't enough and thought they were entitled to luxury in the face of poverty. No amount of volunteering at a homeless shelter was going to change the fundamental problems of entitled greed. So I struggled with what to do until I heard a still small voice that was and was not my own ask, "What have you been called to do?"

I did not immediately say yes to ministry. It was a long, painful process of discernment. It was solitary at first because I wanted to be sure; if I was going to upend my life, then it had to be my own decision. When I shared my call with friends and family, I was lovingly and sometimes jokingly affirmed ("Oh, that explains things—you've been preaching"). It was especially important that my sister affirmed my call.

The process of becoming a Unitarian Universalist minister is not an easy one. Seminary challenged me in ways I could not have expected. I went into seminary thinking I knew what I believed and left it believing in something totally different, and totally my own. It helped me make peace with the faith of my childhood, and it was then that I truly became a Unitarian Universalist. And the credentialing process was not easy either. It was not designed by or for People of Color so I had to navigate a system meant for white people, in particular white cisgender men. But I survived it, and made it through to eventually accepting a call to parish ministry.

In the years I have served in congregations, I have never regretted listening to the call of my soul into ministry. You learn to love the people where you are serving, and you must always remember whom or what you are serving (hint: it's not the people of the congregation). There are tender moments when someone shares with you their burdens and you help make a hard time a little easier. There are joyful moments when you welcome new life into the congregation. There are boring moments when you have to go to one more meeting. There are prideful moments when you experience your congregation growing in new and sometimes unexpected ways. It is not an easy profession. It is full of heartbreak—people you love die, yet it is the best profession if you have the heart for it.

For a Black woman, ministry can be particularly stressful. It's the microaggressions and sometimes macroaggressions that make it so difficult. One of the more disappointing aspects of ministry has been the lack of support from women, Black and white, in the congregations I have served. I have heard this same observation from my white women colleagues as well. Women, it seems, have not been acculturated into being comfortable with their own authority and power. This internalized oppression is often directed toward women who are in positions of authority. It is something I hope the next generations of women ministers will not have to confront.

Surviving Ministry

All ministers must develop practices that keep them grounded and emotionally, spiritually, and physically healthy. The demands of ministry are great, greater than many other professions. One hour of work in ministry is the equivalent of three hours of work in my corporate life. We are expected to give of our minds, our spirits, and our bodies. And often Black women are asked to give more time to endeavors beyond their congregations with little regard for the toll that may also take. We, Black women, need to learn to develop a spiritual practice of "No" less lest we find ourselves constantly exhausted.

My survival in ministry is possible because I have several practices to keep me grounded. I keep a practice that every day before I leave my office, I remember that moment of the day when I know why I said yes to ministry. It may have been for thirty seconds out of a ten-hour day, but it is there. And that is what I try to remember of my day. It helps me look forward to the next day with anticipation and not dread.

I also have a spirit buddy I speak with five mornings a week at 8:30, just to check in on how our spirits are doing. This is one of the most important things in my life. We check in on our spiritual practices to make sure that we have some accountability. And we ask each other, "What is your intention for your spirit today? How are you? How is your spirit?" In the most difficult of times, the friendship of other people, particularly other ministers, is essential. You can't do this alone.

It is also important for ministers of color to have white colleagues whom they trust. Sometimes we think what we are experiencing is because we are not white when in truth it is because we are ministers. Having trusted white colleagues helps us to know what is happening because of our calling and what is happening because of our race.

I'm also part of a small group of women ministers that we call the Dirty Dog Laundry. We're just five women ministers of color who meet on Zoom since we're scattered all around the country. We share our laughter and our tears, our hopes and our fears. It's important to make these relationships and keep them. And when you are asked for something, you say yes because you one day will have to ask. These relationships help you survive ministry.

Finally, I try to make sure to attend gatherings of colleagues of color, such as Finding Our Way Home. It is reinvigorating to be in a space where you don't have to explain what and how you are feeling. It is good to be with people who are sharing the same struggle.

In the end, the same things that helped us survive the faith are the same things that help us survive ministry in this faith—being spiritually grounded, having friends and allies, and just the right amount of patience.

The Journey Ends

One day I will complete my journey in ministry and ultimately in life. I'd like someone to say, "She was a pain in the butt (especially about her middle initial), but she was kind. She was committed. She had a vision. Sometimes she worked hard, but not every day." We never know what our legacy will be. I hope that what I have within Unitarian Universalism will survive and thrive without me. I hope I helped to put us on a path toward building something that has never been, a world where no one is in the center and no one is on the margins. A faith that lives up to its highest aspirations. I hope we are willing to experiment and try and fail and try and fail and try and fail, getting a little bit closer every time. I am unafraid of our failure. I am more afraid that we won't take the risk.

When I achieved final (full) fellowship, I wasn't planning to go to General Assembly that year. Elizabeth, my wife, said I had to go. "Someone has to see that a Black woman can attain this," she told me. As it turned out, I was the only Black woman who was getting final (full) fellowship that year. Black people in the audience came up to me, people I had never seen before, and told me how wonderful it was just to see me.

I don't know if I've had an impact for any young ministers of color, but I know that it made a difference for me to see the possibilities of Black women as ministers, and as powerful ministers. I am so grateful to all of those brave women for paving the way. It wasn't easy for me, but it wasn't as hard as it was for them. I really am so grateful, and so sad and angry sometimes at how poorly our faith treated them. I owe my ministerial mothers a debt of gratitude that I cannot repay except perhaps through my own ministry and passing it forward.

I am a Black, lesbian, woman, Unitarian Universalist minister. And I am a person first.

I Am Still Here!

REV. DR. QIYAMAH A. RAHMAN
PRELIMINARY FELLOWSHIP 2008,
FULL FELLOWSHIP 2013

My call to ministry has been a lifelong one. My grandfather was a Baptist minister, but it was really my mother and grandmother who provided a spiritual foundation and served as role models for me. My grandmother recognized my budding spirituality and encouraged me. We had children's prayer services at her house in the summertime. I would invite my little friends over and lead them in Bible study. I read from the Bible and interpreted scripture, and we sang songs mimicking the adults from church. Looking back, they probably came more for the refreshments my grandmother served and to get out of the sweltering Detroit sun.

Jesus was one of my early teachers and role models. Jesus related to the poor, the disabled, and other marginalized groups and encouraged female disciples. He preached love. The good and virtuous character of Jesus resonated with me, and I felt a kindred spirit and the desire to be good. It felt very natural, like it was an extension of who I was. Doing good and being good brought out the best in me. Learning about compassion and justice tapped into what I believe is the inherent goodness of children. These teachings inspired me and developed my moral foundation and permanently influenced my life.

The first Unitarian Universalist Principle affirms the "inherent worth and dignity of all people." I learned that lesson early in my life from my mother. She reprimanded me one day when I sent away a vagrant who knocked at our door asking for money when I was around ten years old. She made me run up the street and bring him back to the house when she discovered what had happened. When he returned, she gave him some money. We were poor, but she taught me a lesson about sharing and giving to those less fortunate. Because she interpreted the Bible literally, she reminded me that the stranger I had just turned away could be an angel in disguise. The belief in angelic beings looking to catch humans doing good was reinforced as a result of that incident. I still believe in angels. But I know that we are the angels, just as we are the "devil/evil" that we fear.

Sunday was a day of worship and rest. Worship was a family affair. When I was growing up, everyone in my family attended church with the exception of my father, who I was convinced was going to hell. Our lives were all bound together by the powerful rituals of Bible stories, Sunday School, worship, food, Sunday visits, and rides in our very crowded family car. Looking back, I now know that church was a refuge from the day-to-day struggle of being Black in America. As a child, I thought it was simply about playing and being with my friends. The soul-stirring gospel choir's melodic voices filled the small storefront church of Greater St. Stephens Missionary Baptist Church and reached deep inside us to pull out the bittersweet stuff of life that made it possible for the adults to keep on keeping on. Church was the world Black folks created to escape white folks and the degradation of oppression and life's adversities. The titles—Reverend, Mr. and Mrs., Sister and Brother— were their efforts to dignify their lives, to honor themselves in the midst of white America's vicious dishonoring. According to Anthony Pinn, Black Unitarian Universalist scholar and author, Black people's emphasis on "adornment," style, and dressing "to the nines" represents our "hermeneutics of style" and exemplifies Black efforts to heal from the effects of oppression.[32] Pinn points to the "ebb and flow of the Black creative

32 Anthony Pinn's books include the following: *Terror and Triumph: The Nature of Black Religion; Why, Lord?: Suffering and Evil in Black Theology; Varieties of African American Religious Experience; Fortress Introduction to Black Church History* (co-authored with Anne H. Pinn); and *Loving the Body: Black Religious Studies and the Erotic* (co-edited with Dwight N. Hopkins).

impulse and the values and sensibilities that . . . understand(s) the content of Black cultural expression and history as devices of transformation."[33]

Church was a world totally set apart from the rest of the week. The unmistakable vocal inflections and southern cadences of Baptist preaching stirred the passions and exhorted the emotions. Many Black ministers worked full time in various occupations during the week and were transformed on Sunday by their calls to ministry and impassioned worship styles. Church was where I made my first speech and claimed my first accolades as a public speaker. It was where I conducted my first meeting, held my first office, and experienced the surrogate parenting of the extended church family. The adults routinely inquired about my grades and academic performance. The community set high standards and expectations for all the children in the church. We were expected to achieve and make a contribution to our community and to society and to "make something" of ourselves. Many of the elderly members did not possess formal education and were thus fiercely insistent that young people get what they didn't. They all had a profound influence on my religious, personal, and intellectual development.

My paternal grandmother, Lucinda Howard, was a strong influence in my life. She attended a sanctified church, pastored by Elder Winan, the ancestor of the now famous gospel-singing Winans. I often accompanied my grandmother to church. I was captivated by the regalness of the older women who kissed and greeted one another with titles of Sister So-and-So and Mother So-and-So. The various musical instruments fascinated me and included snare drums, guitars, and a piano. The Holiness Church subscribed to the Bible's proclamation to "make a joyful noise unto the Lord." As these elderly women stood up to testify, their mesmerizing oratorical skills captivated me. "Dear Saints," they would say,

---

33 Anthony Pinn, *Terror and Triumph: The Nature of Black Religion* (Minneapolis: Fortress Press, 2003), 141-146.

I give thanks for waking up this morning, clothed in my right mind and with the activity of my limbs. I am thankful that my bed was not my cooling board. Praise God. I'm so glad that trouble don't last always. And that one day I heard a small voice that said, "Come unto me all ye that labor and are heavy burdened and I will give you rest." It didn't matter that I was living a life of sin. It didn't matter that I was a backslider. There is someone who hears your cries in the midnight hour, someone whose sweet name is Jesus.

By then the mothers, that is, the elder women of the church, would have begun to speak in tongues. Others might be dancing, possessed by the Holy Spirit. Their passion and the electrifying synergy of the instruments would pick up the rhythm of the people's graceful and passionate movements, along with their electrically charged words. Memories of my grandmother and others at the Pentecostal Church inspire me even years later because they bestowed on me the passion and authenticity that informed their relationship with the sacred and divine. Their God was alive and real in their lives.

My grandmother also took me to the local Catholic Church with her Mexican friend Lydia. The neighborhood that I was raised in, Cork Town, was the oldest neighborhood in Detroit, and it had originally been settled by Irish immigrants. When the Irish moved out, Black people and other poor people and people of color moved in. My community resembled the United Nations; it was a mixture of Southern whites and Southern blacks, Maltese people, Puerto Ricans, Mexicans, Polish people, and others from the Old World. Many of these elders only spoke their native tongues. The racial and cultural diversity was a gift that influenced me as I began the early stages of my ministry of interfaith outreach.

I experienced my "God is dead" period shortly after I began college in the 1960s at Wayne State University in Detroit. I was the first and still the only one of my siblings to complete a four-year college degree. The "strong" religious foundation that had nurtured me in my early years was inadequate in this new juncture of my life. I was becoming a thinking human being capable of analysis and drawing my own conclusions. My great passions were the Cuban and African revolutions, the civil rights movement, and the Black Power movement. I had trouble reconciling social justice with organized religion because I had not yet been exposed to Black liberation theology. Also, I did not understand or make a distinction between spirituality and organized religion; I did not realize that what I was resisting was organized religion and not my spirituality. I threw the proverbial baby out with the bathwater and embraced the Black power movement and Marxism-Leninism with a passion. Furthermore, it seemed incongruent to worship a dead white man hanging on a cross who had gone to heaven and left us to fend for ourselves. The intellectuals at Wayne State University captured my imagination and stimulated my young and fertile mind. In my mind, the atheists and agnostics were the most vocal and articulate of them and made the most sense. I imagine that if there had been a UU campus ministry, I might have become a Unitarian Universalist much sooner.[34] I was eighteen, young, naïve, unsure of myself, and exploring life; now that I had disavowed values that were foundational to me, my world turned upside down. The insurrection of Black people in the 1960s, my working class background, and my strong Christian leanings toward social justice all shaped my solidarity with oppressed peoples and my desire to engage in justice work. These same factors have also influenced my desire to pursue ministry. My calling has always been aligned with oppressed peoples.

Growing up in a violent household greatly impacted my life and my future ministry. Just as having a disabled sibling inspired me as a social

---

34 Little did I know that there was a UU congregation within walking distance from campus. —QR

worker, growing up in a violent household motivated me to work on women's empowerment and peace building. I believed then, as I do now, that I have a message of hope and renewal to share. My transformation has come about through my individual healing, derived from my social justice work over the years and many other sources. You might say that I know a little about healing from the trauma of violence.

After September 11, 2001, I asked myself, "Had I been one of the ones who had died, what would I have regretted not having done?" What I heard was "not going into the ministry." Shortly afterward, I began the Modified Residency Program at Meadville Lombard Theological School in January 2003.

Passed Through the Fire

One of the most challenging periods of my life as a UU that impacted my journey toward ministry occurred during my tenure as a district executive, co-employed by the UUA and the Southern District, formerly known as the Thomas Jefferson District. I began serving in that position on July 1, 1999. Six years later, I was negotiating my resignation. This experience propelled me toward ministry in a very unexpected way. The experience leading up to my resignation tested me to my very core and tapped reservoirs of strength that even I did not know I possessed.

Becoming the district executive was the culmination of several years of lay leadership and social justice work as a Unitarian Universalist. The position melded my devotion to social justice and my love of Unitarian Universalism. Several years into my tenure, I had enrolled in the Modified Residency Program at Meadville Lombard Theological School. One of the ministers in my district called me and informed me that he was dating a congregant whom he had previously counseled. He assured me the counseling relationship had concluded. According to our Code of Conduct at that time, a minister could date congregants if they were both single. He indicated that he did not want me to hear this from someone else. Sometime later, I received a request from him and his board for a congregational consultation. In the process of doing an assessment and conducting interviews, I discovered that the minister had been dating a member who had been married to an abusive spouse. And that she had left the church and that he was now dating someone else in the congregation. I felt this information needed to be included in my consultant's report to the Board. I checked in with field staff. I was of the opinion that I should write two separate reports, one for the Board with a more detailed report on my findings and another that did not include this information for the congregation. Field staff felt one report was appropriate. My overextended schedule forced me to write and prepare the report in a time frame that found me composing it right up until the time I was scheduled to present my findings to the Board. I recall requesting the use of their copy machine so that I could make sufficient copies for the Board members and the minister. I remember an awkward moment when I encountered the minister in question and handed him a copy of the report with a statement to the effect that I had felt it necessary to include information about his relationship with a congregation member.

At that point I had already made two major errors, not getting in touch with the minister's good officer to apprise him of the situation and not providing the minister with a copy of the report well in advance. To make matters worse, there were a couple of people present at the Board meeting who were not members of the Board. In hindsight, I should have requested a closed session. What was I thinking? I wasn't. As it turned out, they didn't care that their minister was having an affair with a married member. They were actually angry at me for disclosing this information. And they did not have an issue with the minister. Months later, the minister would be terminated by the same Board for lying to them about some other matter.

The morning after the Board meeting, my phone rang and the president of the Board said he was not going to be able to meet with me because he didn't feel "safe" with me. I remember thinking, *This big white male is feeling unsafe with me?* Imagine how I felt last night in the midst of a Board meeting that became hostile toward me because I disclosed unprofessional behavior about their minister. This was an instance in which a powerful white male usurped language to play the victim and to name me as the abuser. As word got around about what had transpired, some of the ministers in the district were so angry they demanded that I be removed. From the very beginning, I took responsibility for my errors, publicly and privately. Initially, I thought that things would settle down and I would be able to recover from my mishandling of the situation. However, a group of ministers were not willing to let it go. Over time, I began to realize that I had compromised my credibility by my mishandling of the situation and that I was not going to be able to recover and effectively serve the district. I was waking up to emails and petitions demanding my resignation several times a week. I asked for reconciliation efforts with the minister and good officer, none of which were successful. I apologized in a telephone conversation between a UUA mediator, myself, the minister in question, and his good officer. While I do not remember whether they accepted my apology or not, I do recall that they still insisted on my removal. I turned to several individuals for consultation. One such person was Rev. Dr. Deborah Pope Lance. We both agreed that while I had committed administrative errors, I was not guilty of misconduct. But the minister was, and I was being treated like the misconductor. At that time, the UUA was supportive and standing with me. However, once the congregational Board threatened certain actions, I acquiesced rather than jeopardize the UUA and force a showdown between the congregation and the UUA. Practically, I knew I could not expect the UUA to stand up for one Black female employee at the risk of losing several hundred members along with their fair share contribution. So I reluctantly negotiated my resignation.

When I announced my resignation at a large gathering, I remember looking out over the audience into the eyes of the minister in question, knowing that he knew he had won. Rev. Nan Hobart had called me and invited me to shift from the Modified Residency Program that I had been enrolled in and to transition to full-time status. It was one of the darkest times of my UU life. Her invitation and my relocation to Chicago were the best things that could have happened to me. I needed to get out of Dodge. So I put my house up for sale in Charlotte, North Carolina; sold or gave away all my possessions; packed my sedated cat; stuffed clothes and books into my Prius; and drove from Charlotte to Chicago non-stop to begin my life as a full-time seminarian at age fifty-nine.

While I was surprised at the level of racism and sexism displayed by the white male ministers, I was more astonished at the depths of my internalized oppression. Some of my drive as a district executive was motivated by the need to prove that I was as good as any of the white staff. I was the second district executive of color and the first Black woman to serve in that capacity. My overfunctioning, rooted in my internalized oppression, got me in trouble when I eventually overextended

I continued to expand programs and services in the district to demonstrate what a great district we were and to show how smart and capable I was, all to prove that I was not an affirmative action hire. Of course I was not consciously processing any of this at the time. So what did I learn? I learned that I am stronger than I realized.

myself. I continued to expand programs and services in the district to demonstrate what a great district we were and to show how smart and capable I was, all to prove that I was not an affirmative action hire. Of course I was not consciously processing any of this at the time.

So what did I learn? I learned that I am stronger than I realized. I was given a six-month severance package. I used that time to complete my dissertation on clergy sexual misconduct titled "By the Shores of Babylon We Wept: The Institutional Response of the Unitarian Universalist Association to Clergy Sexual Misconduct between 1995 and 2005." And I worked to heal the internalized oppression that had affected me so disastrously and deeply that it caused me to sabotage my life. I worked to forgive those who were hell-bent on destroying me. I have evolved into a healthier and more whole human being because of the experience, and it has instilled a message of hope and renewal in my ministry.

Community or Parish Ministry?

My ministerial career could be divided into two phases, my time as a community minister and my time in parish ministry. Although separate tracks no longer exist for parish and community ministry, there are still distinctions. From 2008 to 2012, I served as the director of contextual ministry and senior lecturer with Meadville Lombard Theological School. Because of my extensive background in domestic violence, I expected to continue to use my training as a master's level social worker and minister. I completed a chaplain's residency at Carolina Medical Center instead of a parish internship. When I came before the Ministerial Fellowship Committee, they deemed it necessary that I also do a parish internship. This decision reflects the prioritization of parish ministry. I am not aware of any instance in which a seminarian pursuing parish ministry has been required to do a community ministry internship. I point this out as one of the ways the Unitarian Universalist Ministers Association and the Ministerial Fellowship Committee continue to hold parish ministry as the standard while relegating community ministry to second class status.

I spent five very happy years with Meadville Lombard identified as a community minister. When Meadville discontinued its residential program, my position was greatly impacted. One of my favorite duties was serving as community liaison, identifying local organizations engaged in the most effective social change work. I would arrange internships for our residential students. In hindsight, I realized these site leaders inspired me as I was in relationship with some of the most dynamic and successful activists and organizations in the Chicago area. They were teaching me and our students by example. Meanwhile, the modified residency students selected their own local sites. The relationships between these local site supervisors and myself were not as strong because I was only able to engage them via telephone and written reports. Because of financial constraints, site visits were not possible. I found myself increasingly in my office, at my desk, in front of my computer, and on the telephone. I realized that I was no longer happy in my work, my ministry. I had not gone to seminary to sit in an office. I had always had a penchant for travel and a fascination with Unitarian congregations outside the country. I would visit their websites and fantasize about these far off places. I wanted to live and work outside the United States.

So when an announcement appeared on the website of the Unitarian Universalist Fellowship of St. Croix (UUFSC) for a guest minister, I immediately applied. In February 2012, I flew to St. Croix, Virgin Islands, to serve as their guest minister. The second week I was on island, I knew I was supposed to live and work there. I have never had such a compelling feeling. In the short time that I was there, I connected with the non-profits conducting education and advocacy on interfaith activities, domestic violence, and sexual assault issues. With them and with the Unitarian Universalist community there, I had found my people.

At the conclusion of my four weeks, I told the Board members of the UUFSC that I would be returning and that while they were under no obligation to me, I would be happy to talk about serving as their minister if they were interested. On July 1, 2012, I landed on St. Croix. I had packed and shipped some of my books and clothes and my car. I had shipped multiple boxes through the U.S. mail. I sold and gave away all my furnishings. This was reminiscent of my decision to transition from the Modified Residency Program to the full-time Residential Program.

Life in St. Croix

When I arrived in St. Croix, I moved into a small cottage that a member of the Fellowship had graciously offered for my use. I lived there until I obtained a place of my own almost three months later, when I found employment. My faith was so strong and my focus so clear about my vision to live and work in St. Croix. I recall that when Rev. Dr. Lee Barker, then president of Meadville Lombard, inquired what my plan B would be if things did not work out in St. Croix, I confidently replied, "I don't need a plan B." And I didn't.

I began work the first week in September as the medical social worker at the Caribbean Kidney Center. The position was full time and my parish ministry was about quarter time. For the first time in my ministerial career, I was serving as both parish and community minister simultaneously. I made the decision to change my status from community minister to parish ministry with the UUA. While I considered the duties of a medical social worker as ministry, I knew my employers would not necessarily view it as such. However, now that I am serving as a disaster case manager, it may be time to entertain that conversation with the Ministerial Fellowship Committee. Being in final fellowship gives me plenty of leverage, and it may even be a moot issue.

Congregations have their personalities. UUFSC was 99 percent white and social justice-oriented. Members were heavily involved in various justice issues but tended not to identify themselves as Unitarian Universalists in these activities. I, on the other hand, made a point of letting everyone know I was Rev. Qiyamah with the UUFSC. I knew the high visibility I was achieving conveyed our values and demonstrated our "faith in action," something I could never convey to congregants. The Fellowship's physical location on St. Croix contributed to its isolation. The Fellowship started off in the living room of one of the founders. Thirty years later, they were still behaving like the small-sized congregation they were. The congregational culture reflected the traditional family-sized congregation, which tends to be a closed system based on its size. Congregational life therefore tends to revolve around itself for its survival.

The Fellowship possessed an introverted personality. For instance, they did not want visitors to stand up and be recognized. They also did not want new members to come up front and be recognized in a ceremony. I did make those changes, but I tried not to push them too fast or too hard since I was still new and in my first year.

Making Change in Ministry

I began at UUFSC as their first paid minister in their almost twenty-nine-year history. Surprisingly, there were no major changes in those six years. But not because I did not desire to make changes. Rev. Ken Hurto, then the regional executive, stated when conducting board development in conjunction with my installation that the minister should not make any major changes early on. A member reminded me of this when I added prayer/reflection/meditation to the Order of Service. I added it, and except for her comment, there was no pushback. I also added a "welcome" time during which the congregation would exchange greetings. After service, one of the matriarchs approached me and informed me that if I did that again, she would not return. I didn't, and she stayed! Choose your battles. While I was offended that she would threaten me with her departure, it was too early in my settlement to do battle with the matriarch. However, the same individual informed me after I preached my epic Easter sermon that it was perfect except for the boring title, "A UU Perspective on Easter." I wish she were alive to hear my "Last Seven Words of Jesus" sermon.

Some of my sermon topics were generated by concrete needs and questions from members, including the following:

- Why do you have to end your talks with "Blessed be"?

- Why do you insist on calling it *worship*? We shouldn't be worshipping anything.

- After the Kwanzaa service, one of the Humanists quizzed me about whether I should be condoning socialism, in reference to Ujamaa, which translates as *collective economics*.

- Another time, an individual left because "it's too much like church." This same individual came back several months later. We never had a conversation about it. I warmly welcomed her back. She learned what many of us already know, that many join for the sense of community and connection and not necessarily for theology.

Almost all of the changes I was able to make in the Fellowship were small changes. The congregational culture was pretty set around things like meeting schedules. Some of the small changes I was able to make included the schedule for the congregational year. As snowbirds, most of the leadership left St. Croix for the summer. As a result, UUFSC did not begin the new congregational year until October. Most congregations begin in September. This was an easy fix and one they did not resist since they now had a minister on board in charge of worship.

There were big changes that I wanted to make but was not able to, starting with the worship schedule. Every consultant who had ever met with the leadership of UUFSC told them that they needed to meet every Sunday instead of every other Sunday. In all fairness to the congregation, they had a longstanding covenant group that met on alternate Sundays at the same time that worship started on the other Sundays. I immediately knew I would not be successful in getting them to change this schedule. In the six years that I served as minister, I attended the covenant group fewer than six times. This was because I knew I did not want to endorse the covenant group usurping the worship slot in the schedule, but I also knew that I was not going to be successful in getting them to change up. It was part of their culture and as popular as Sunday services. I felt they should be having worship service. I was smart enough to recognize this was not a battle I could win.

Closing down over the summer was another part of the Fellowship's culture that I was unable to change. It went back to the Fellowship's founding. Even my offer to conduct Sunday services May through August with no pay and to use recorded music didn't change their minds. When I first arrived, I spent the off Sundays visiting other places of worship. Since I was not attending the covenant group, it would have been too easy to fall into a pattern of sleeping in or gardening, which was my favorite, on my Sundays off.

Building trust, expanding membership, and growing the vision and mission were goals that I worked on with the Fellowship. It is far too easy to become parochial and to create policy and procedures based on convenience rather than vision.

Ministerial Agency and Authority

Being the Fellowship's first paid minister could have been an absolute disaster. We worked amazingly well together despite that history. But the history included the ordination of a member who had never had any formal seminary training, which posed a challenge to my authority. Serving as a worship associate does not a pastor make. However, the only time this became an issue was when one of our matriarchs died. I was not invited to conduct the memorial service. I was too new to parish ministry to fully realize I had been dissed, but I knew that as minister, I should have conducted the service. The family might not have known, but the individual who was ordained without training should have known. At no point did she approach me, even though we helped to provide pastoral care and assisted the hospice staff during the last days of the deceased. The Covenant Group and I worked together to prepare some reflections that they asked me to present. I believe the Fellowship, for the most part, did not consider it an oversight or disrespectful. But in retrospect, I realize that it was a reflection of their ambivalence about pastoral agency and authority, as was the fact that out of the two Sundays devoted to worship, one of them was reserved for me and the other for a community speaker. And ambivalence about my role and value was also demonstrated when a budget-tightening period resulted in a proposed reduction of my salary. My annual salary was already less than $10,000. But the Fellowship retained the guest speaker's budget with no cuts in the number of Sundays for guest speakers. My original salary was eventually restored due to my protests, but for the first time, I was beginning to question whether the long time without a paid minister was due less to a lack of available ministers and more to ambivalence about a minister's presence and authority.

Neighbor to Neighbor

As a minister, I have married and buried folks. I have sat at the bedside of dying individuals as they breathed their last breath. I have listened to pain so devasting that I wept, sometimes silently and sometimes out loud. I have sometimes wondered if I were good enough, and whole enough, to wear the title of Reverend. Many times, I have reflected aloud about the goodness of my life and the great fortune to be a vessel of the Most High and to read, study, and write about spirituality while I stumble and fumble along the path that I have chosen.

The greatest accomplishment by far in my ministry was conceiving and birthing the nonprofit Neighbor to Neighbor (N2N) after a Category 5 hurricane devastated the Virgin Islands. Nothing in my ministry until that time called forth all that is whole, visionary, and prophetic in me more than the creation of N2N. And even with all the heartbreak I endured when I had to walk away from it, I believe it was a milestone in my now twelve-year ministry career. N2N represented a level of faith that I held yet rarely demonstrated in my life. I experienced the single-mindedness of a servant leader. I knew that the manifestation of N2N was not of this world and not of my doing, but came from something greater than me. There is a power in that kind of knowing, accompanied by the belief that no obstacle is too great to overcome when the task is spirit-driven. The joy derived from serving and being a vessel of the Most High is impossible to describe. I was living my unique purpose. It was why I became a minister. It was why I became UU; the sense of healing and transforming the world is the ultimate high.

In my earlier years, my life was about making do, surviving, hiding out from myself and others, and healing as I grew strong enough to stand in the slowly revealing truth of my humanity and worth.

I am now determined to stand in the power of my truth, though I am sometimes afraid—afraid to not truly live my greatness, yet knowing something greater than myself brought me through the tumultuous times. I cannot help but believe in an existence beyond myself; what I call that has changed over time as I evolved and transformed. My life has become a journey of faith, of trial and error. I have seen and experienced the unexplainable and reveled in transcendent moments that have carried me out of harm's way many a time. Words cannot describe the dragons I have slayed nor those I have been rescued from to arrive at this point. My survival is a miracle, and I am not supposed to look this good after all I have been through. I've still got some mess, but I am truly blessed! And for this I am thankful.

Wade in the Water

REV. DR. NATALIE MAXWELL FENIMORE
PRELIMINARY FELLOWSHIP 2011,
FULL FELLOWSHIP 2015

I was in my early twenties when I began attending a Unitarian Universalist Church in Maryland. I had never heard of Unitarian Universalism, but I was partnered with someone who had grown up as a Unitarian and had sought out the local church for himself, and then for us in 1980.

My partner was, and is, white, and so were seemingly all the other people who came to my first local Unitarian Universalist church, even though there was, and is, an African American community a couple of blocks away from the church. This town was founded in slavery days. This free Black community was defiantly named Haiti.

But there I was, in a new community, in new relationships. I was a young adult Black woman who had moved away from inner-city, working class, Detroit. I was in this Unitarian Universalist faith community, enclosed in a white, middle-class, suburban reality. I might have drowned in this new and unfamiliar place, but it turned out that there were white grandmas who treated me much like Black grandmas would have. These women welcomed me and showed me around the church. They may have been amazed at themselves for doing so; I was myself amazed that they did. They sometimes let it out that I surprised them by being well spoken and educated and intellectually curious. I sometimes let it out that I was surprised at how little they knew about non-white people. But most of them and I grew together and became close. Some of these church women sewed my ordination stole more than twenty years later.

The welcome was harder to come by from some of the white male leaders in the congregation. As I became more involved in the church and started to ask questions about why things were done the way they were or asked if some changes might make the church more welcoming to non-whites and those from working class backgrounds, I actually had white men in the congregation telling me, "If you do not like the church the way it is, then maybe this is not the church for you. You should leave." I did not leave. I did decide to learn more about Unitarian Universalism.

Growing up in Detroit, I had not been either particularly political or engaged with organized religion. Both politics and religion swirled around me, and although I had little specific or personal involvement in organized politics or institutional religion, I soaked up what was in the atmosphere in a general way. My community was filled to bursting with the patterns and the sounds of the African American Baptist Church. Storefront churches popped up all the time. The Gospel Choir at my high school had auditorium performances where people spoke in tongues and fell out in the spirit.

But I seem to have "inherited" my mother's distrust and skepticism of organized religion. My mother experienced a church leadership both in Alabama and Detroit that did not value, support, or protect girl children or women—and she pointed this out to me. She and I both shared an aversion to prosperity gospel, which seemed to expand economic disparities in the Black community and not serve to expand communal economic growth or opportunities. So while I read and studied about religion, by the time I was in my early teens, I was not a church-goer. I was not even a Christmas and Easter attendee.

My family came from Alabama at the end of the Great Migration and our focus was on work and economic opportunity, communal and personal survival. My family gave me the task of getting good grades, graduating high school, and getting a scholarship to take me out of

Detroit and off to college. I did not go to political rallies or marches or know much about the labor history of my town, and so I did not know anything about the Unitarians in Detroit who were involved in working for social change. I did not know about Viola Liuzzo, the white Unitarian Detroiter who was murdered in Selma, Alabama, in 1965 while working for civil rights for Black people. Growing up, I only knew about my neighborhood's growing poverty, crime, unemployment, and influx of drugs. My task was to get away and I did, carrying great sorrow for the good things I was leaving, as well as grief for the passing of the city of Detroit as I knew it.

The Unitarian Universalists I came to be a part of in the Joseph Priestley District were very focused on social justice. It was central to their congregational and individual identities. And my presence in their community as a youngish Black woman with a working class urban background seemed to affirm, for the congregation its welcoming liberalism.

However, it was theology that held me in Unitarian Universalism. The Unitarian Universalist Principles represented a faith community where inquiry, dissent, lack of group-think, and individuality were encouraged, which I found interesting and challenging. Congregationalism was something I found dear to me. In congregationalism, I see an affirmation of the importance of each person in a faith community, the importance of each person in life. I did not want popes, bishops, or authoritarian ministers.

I also found myself opened up to intersectionality as a Unitarian Universalist. The belief in the inherent worth and dignity of all people and the interconnected web led me to reject the theological basis of anti-LGBTQ+ and the history of ignoring women's religious leadership. Unitarian Universalism challenged me to dig some of the "Old Ways" of the Black Church out of me at the same time that I continue to cherish the deep spiritual and communal dimension of the faith of my upbringing. I moved, and am still moving, to align my heart with the pluralist, caring, Beloved Community that our Association aspires to become. The Association is not there yet, and neither am I, but we aspire.

At my Unitarian Universalist home church, I became a congregational lay leader almost by accident. I was doing things around the church like cooking for the summer brunches, working at the Bazaar, and teaching religious education. On some level, doing these things came from my Black community "church lady" model. I saw that there were things to be done for the community and I almost always said yes to volunteer opportunities. I have since learned to say no.

Eventually, I was asked to join the church Board. At the first Board organizing retreat, the facilitator had us engage in a team-building exercise. We were to talk about how we would work together to plan a camping trip. I said, "Why camping? Does everybody on the Board have to love camping? What about city-loving people?" It felt to me like all those experience-based questions on standardized tests that mistook background knowledge for intelligence. I really felt on the outs after that and only spent one year on the Board.

I found a "better fit" in the wider Unitarian Universalist Association, specifically in the Joseph Priestley District (JPD). I went to programs and workshops, so many that I cannot remember them all. I served on the JPD Board, and the Journey Toward Wholeness Committee. It was while serving on a JPD executive search committee that I first met Rev. Bill Sinkford. He had come, as the director of congregational life, to assist with the search. Until that point, I had not met a Black UUA official at that level. I remember realizing this at the moment, realizing that it had not occurred to me that the person coming from the UUA might be Black. As I remember it, Rev. Sinkford met me with the same surprise and pleasure in my Blackness.

Having become a member of a Unitarian Universalist congregation in 1982 and then a first-time parent in 1984, I found myself most immersed in the Unitarian Universalist religious education community.

I can clearly remember the day I was drawn to consider a career in Unitarian Universalist religious education. I was volunteering in a second-grade classroom, telling the story of the Exodus as found in the Hebrew Bible. As I was telling the story, I felt a deep desire to connect the children in my class to the Exodus story, as I had been connected to its' themes of freedom and justice in the Black community.

But there was a gulf there in the room. These white, middle-class, suburban children and I were born into different worlds. What did their souls need to be liberated from? At the time, I felt the distance even from these very young white children. I also felt the desire to bridge the distance.

It must have been at least two or three years after my "Exodus" experience that I quit my job and took a part-time position as a Unitarian Universalist religious education director in a congregation near my home church.

The decision to become a religious professional was a surprise to me. As I have already written, I did not grow up in a particularly religious family. I had not grown up wanting to or imagining that I would work in a church. My birth family was skeptical and confused.

As a UU religious educator, I found a talented and supportive collegial community. These were the members of the Liberal Religious Educators Association. This group was almost all female. They often felt sidelined in the decision-making in the congregations where they worked. They were often called the "cookies and crayons ladies"—and that was not a compliment. The reality was and is that they were a force of nature and central to keeping Unitarian Universalism alive. Becoming one of them changed my life.

The Unitarian Universalist religious education community was a sisterhood for me. I met generous, dedicated professionals, colleagues, and friends. I also heard stories about directors of religious education (DREs) setting their skirts on fire while lighting the chalice in

Children's Chapel. I had to call parents when Coming of Age children threw rocks at squirrels in Boston Common and the police got involved. I got to connect Black UU youth with YRUU. I had a Korean American parent tell me how she appreciated my telling her child about Korean Lunar New Year traditions that she had set aside in the process of being "Americanized." And I saw, and experienced, the hurt and pain of Black UU religious education professionals finding out that our faith communities are not the promised land. When I began as a DRE, our programs did not have broad representation of diversity; it was to even put up pictures on the walls and bulletin boards of non-whites, or have non-white dolls in the nursery room, or have non-white story books.

It was in the UU LREDA gatherings that I first met a larger population of Unitarian Universalists of color. Still, most of the religious professionals were white women. I became the first Black woman president of the Liberal Religious Educators Association in 2011 (serving through 2014). As LREDA president, I was challenged to strengthen the institution, to listen to the concerns of individual religious educators, and to enhance the support for those religious educators. It was wonderful to be on stage as LREDA president for the Service of the Living Tradition at General Assembly to greet both ordained ministers and credentialed religious educators. During my time in LREDA leadership, I was proud to have the UUA Office of Church Finance put in writing that religious educators could receive support from the Living Tradition Fund when they were in need, as do ordained ministers.

The thought of ordained ministry came to me as I worked in religious education. I had been a working religious education professional for almost a decade, and had served as DRE in three congregations when I began to feel that what I was doing was ministry. Many religious education families had already embraced me as a ministerial presence. I believed that I should gain the resources, training, and experience to do my ministry in a way that did as little harm as possible and with as much wisdom and grace as I might be able to hold in my spirit. I started the road to ordination by taking classes part-time and working as a religious educator full-time. There were days when I drove from home to class, and then from class to work, and after work back for another class, and then finally home. But seminary was wonderful, a place of study and community. Once I came off the road and parked in the seminary parking lot because I had noticed that the check oil light was on in the car. I popped the hood and prepared to check the oil. Suddenly I was surrounded by seminarians offering to help; it was a comfort to encounter this "ministry" of care.

And in my United Methodist seminary, I was surrounded by racial, ethnic, cultural, and class diversity. But it was in Unitarian Universalism that I found the theological and spiritual expansiveness that led me away from the fear, homophobia, and capitalist vision of the world that I so often encountered in mainline Christianity.

However, it was hard to get into the "UU Ministers Club." I was not a traditional seminarian. I was older and went to a non-UU seminary, and I had begun as a religious educator. When I first tried to attend the gathering that became Finding Our Way Home, before I was in seminary or ordained, I was told that it was for ministers and not religious educators of color. When I received my UUA religious education credentialing at the master's level, I was able to walk across the stage at the Service of the Living Tradition.

It was years later before all those receiving a credential could be on stage; only the master's level could walk then, and there were only two of us who had received the master's level religious education credential that year. I found myself in the robing room where everyone was preparing, we two lone religious educators among ministers. Watching the greetings and the robing of the ministers, I felt like I was glimpsing a secret insider thing. And then I looked up to see a beautiful Black woman looking at me. She said to me, "Where have you been? I didn't know about you." It was a welcome, a greeting, perhaps an invitation, but also a sadness, a loss, a puzzlement. I was never able to connect with her about this moment and what it meant for me.

I received the Marjorie Bowens-Wheatley scholarship from the UU Women's Federation and a scholarship named for Rev. David Eaton and feel connected to the legacy of these two early Black UU ministers. But I know that there is a missing piece in my development as a Black UU woman minister because I missed knowing so many of the Black UU women elders, the saints, the sisters, the mentors and guides early on. It so often has felt that we were separated from one another. Separated by distance, and our own particular locations within Unitarian Universalism—our seminaries, congregations, regions, specific religious professional identities.

These lost connections haunt me. Now I am myself an elder in the UU religious professionals of color community, and I ask myself what responsibility I have for supporting, sharing, and mentoring newcomers.

As a ministerial intern, I was blessed to be in a congregation where Rev. Carlton Elliott Smith was serving as minister. Carlton and I took many a walk around the block, literally, to process how to navigate the UU ministry as a Black person, microaggressions and all. Carlton mentored and supported me—and made a space for laughter as well. One Christmas Eve, we found ourselves the only ministers on the chancel, two Black ministers and no white people for the first time at the congregation; we turned to each other and laughed.

I have had to struggle against the scarcity model of ministry for Black women in Unitarian Universalism. I have experienced my white colleagues, men and women, presenting to me a "reality" of limited spaces and places for me. They speak, directly and indirectly, of Black pulpits and disrespect for religious education ministry. When I was in search, white colleagues pointed me directly at the associate minister positions in "multi-cultural, diverse" congregations. When I sought positions in congregations that were predominantly white (as most of our UU congregations are) and not led by white ministers trumpeted for their support of diversity, I was met with spoken surprise and negative comments. I also experienced barriers when I sought lead minister positions. The truth was that after my first ministry search, in which I was pre-candidated at multiple congregations, I was offered one position at a small congregation that was considered "diverse" and where a Black minister had served previously.

When I sought positions in congregations that were predominantly white (as most of our UU congregations are) and not led by white ministers trumpeted for their support of diversity, I was met with spoken surprise and negative comments.

White colleagues who had "warned" me that this would happen believed that they were just being "realistic," but they were in reality limiting me, diminishing me. I asked myself if they do this with their white colleagues, or with their ministry colleagues who did not start in religious education? I have talked with white women ministry colleagues, and it seems that there is a competitive and hierarchical nature in our ministry that causes some of these concerns about hierarchy and power for them too.

I have stayed in Unitarian Universalism. I have built a strong and thriving ministry. And when I was last in search, I again applied for a position in a congregation that did not have a history of ministers of color. I was pleased to be approached by white colleagues in religious education asking me to consider the position. I was again supported by Rev. Carlton Smith, who said to me when I hesitated, "There is no one more qualified than you." I was called and became the first minister of color in my current role. The support of my friends and colleagues continues to give me strength and motivates me to explore new areas of ministry.

In 2018, I completed my doctor of ministry degree, completing a long considered subject, how to support positive identity formation for Black Unitarian Universalists. I became a member of the UUA Commission on Institutional Change with the goal of being part of the conversation about how the Unitarian Universalist Association and Unitarian Universalism as a faith will overcome the tragedy of white supremacy culture.

Amazingly, I have now spent more of my life inside Unitarian Universalism than outside. I have not always felt at home. I have not always felt wanted. But I have found a place here, and friends and colleagues whom I hold dear.

Worship:
Co-creating the Sacred Container

REV. JACQUELINE BRETT
PRELIMINARY FELLOWSHIP 2017,
FULL FELLOWSHIP 2021

I think of Jasmine's beautiful long limbs as she dances. Her elongated arms floating up, down, forming curves and arcs as she twirls and leaps, dancing in concert with the others in her company. All of them seeming to float, their skirts twirling, their legs pointing out and up. Them leaping and Jasmine, especially, almost seeming to fly across the floor.

We are silent and rapt in our attention. We are witness to something that touches our hearts as the dancers tell their story, weave in movement and gesture, in posture and facial expressions—all parts of their creative expression of the divine in this space and time we have set aside as a sacred container for worship. We listen to music from the Beloved Community Chorus and we watch the dancers move. Something within me—perhaps it is my divine within—is touched and connected with the energies and movements of these Beautiful Ones here on this Sunday morning sharing the gift of themselves through the story they're creating through movement.

> We have all come,
> now what shall We consciously co-create
> together
> with All That Is
> in All This Awesomeness?
> Note that I did not say accomplish,
> but co-create…

This is Kwanzaa morning, and something is happening in this moment that has not happened on other Kwanzaa mornings, or any other Sunday morning. The room is packed with more people than we usually see, and in particular, more Black people than we have ever seen at one time together with us in our worship space.

When I consider our congregation and all we profess to be, all we aspire to be, I am filled with joy by those in this room, the variegated multitude cramming the seats. I am filled with great joy that the offering before us seems to fill up the eager hearts waiting to celebrate, wanting to know something more about this place—Durham, North Carolina, ancestral land of the Eno and Saponi—wanting to feel affirmed in the possibility of who we in these United States could possibly be, or at least who we in this particular room at this particular time might possibly be.

I am glad that what is being offered and created this Sunday morning seems worthy of the eager hearts in the room. And yet I also feel a sense of mourning and grief that once this Sunday is over, once the beautiful music, dancing, and food of the karamu that will transform our coffee hour into a magnificent feast has ceased, this Sunday's community dispersed, we will become again as we were—white-cultured—like a rubber band that has snapped back to its original shape.

> And so what might we co-create in full embrace of
> this knowing that
>> we are possibility
>> from a sudden burst of light?
>> That we are the light?
> So what might we co-create in the
> love power and wisdom of the
> I Am Spirit
> that is Life?

What Might We Co-Create Together?

I move through the world as a womanist, and have since before it was named a theology—because womanism is simply how we are experiencing and making meaning of the world as Black women. It is the prism through which we are viewing our life experiences, moving through them, and loving and caring for ourselves and our people—all people. We cannot, by the very nature of who we are, change who we are, though we might find ourselves suppressing our natural inclinations to be who we are and bring ourselves completely to wherever we are, thus unwittingly participating in our oppression.

> *I move through the world as a womanist, and have since before it was named a theology—because womanism is simply how we are experiencing and making meaning of the world as Black women. It is the prism through which we are viewing our life experiences, moving through them, and loving and caring for ourselves and our people—all people.*

Worship is my favorite aspect of congregational life, the joining of the gathered community. And my role is to help hold open sacred space, creating the container in which an experience of the holy might enter—however it is experienced—for those who gather. And so creating and offering a worship service, no matter what role I play, is a very precious and sacred practice for me.

I come to worship with my heart wide open, thinking, *What might we co-create together?* in my womanist experiences and understandings, along with everyone else and theirs. And in this I also wonder, *What might the community need today? Pastoral care, ritual, comfort, the warmth of welcome, uplift, agitation, a call to action?*

In our co-creating, we are all challenged by the pluralism of our congregations and the diversity of race, identities, privilege, class, seen and unseen disabilities, and beliefs. What does it mean to shift the focus from the needs of the dominant culture and to consider the needs of all who are in the room, in hopes that not only will all feel their needs have been addressed, but that when people of non-dominant groups show up they might feel compelled to return again because they instinctively sense, *Yes, there is something here for me*?

But co-creating worship requires some moving forward and some moving back. Recognizing that while it's okay for worship to have some structure, the structure might also shift because the gathered community has shifted. So if we are authentically meeting the needs of the gathered body in its entirety, which some of our congregations have said they're eager to see become more diverse, would not worship itself become more diverse as we form Beloved Community?

One thing about being a queer Black woman leading worship is that I am admittedly attuned to the needs of the most marginalized, though I concede that I must address my privilege at times as well. So when Black people, Indigenous people, Latinx, Asian, and other people of color start finding us and decide to return or remain and white folks complain about worship not being like what they've been accustomed to, it's difficult to bear at times. Can't someone else be in the center for a Sunday or even many Sundays? Isn't this space to be shared by all? Black people, Indigenous people, Latinx, Asian, and other people of color often suspend their worship needs and desires and expand their capacity for accepting music and other forms that they might enjoy a little less or feel a little less comfortable with. But the beauty of the sacred container that holds our worship services is in its potential, in its challenge, and in its possibility to hold diverse forms and structures. We don't attempt to do this all at one time, and I am not talking about misappropriating other groups' sacred rituals and forms that have nothing to do with us or in ways that are clearly out of context. I am talking about co-creating worship with integrity, which means that I, as a queer Black clergywoman, can bring the fullness of who I am to the worship experience, while embracing my charge to address the needs of the fully gathered community.

What's Here for Us in This Moment?

I would like to see more people bring curiosity to worship, asking themselves, *What might I learn about this? What's the opportunity for my heart to open in a new way?* as they sit in a service that's not what they expected. Everyone needs this practice: *What's here for me in this moment? Where is the holy for me in all this? Is the sacred not present because I don't care for the music today or someone is shouting Amen or Ashe or clapping their hands—or choosing not to do so?*

I first became curious about Unitarian Universalism when someone in a UU congregation told me they were a humanist. I wondered aloud why they were attending services on Sunday mornings; as soon as the words tumbled out of my mouth I began to question all of my assumptions about what a community of faith was all about, not because of what humanists believed, but because I suddenly became aware of my limiting beliefs. And so I grew curious about the range of beliefs that occupied UU pews on a Sunday morning. I marveled that a theist could sit next to an atheist and be in civil community together. And that a range of beliefs existed between the poles of theism and atheism, and beyond. And that it could all form a community of both/and in faith— however each person defined it. All of this was incomprehensible to me and blew my mind.

And I wanted to know more about Unitarian Universalism because I had never been in such a community of diverse beliefs without folks feeling compelled to condemn one another and to shut out those who did not share their exact beliefs. I had been an evangelical Christian for a period in my life, so I knew something about condemning folks and shutting them out when they didn't believe as I did. But as I allowed myself to expand beyond those limiting beliefs and later discovered Unitarian Universalism, I believed I had found what I had always imagined was possible. And I wanted to be in and live in that possibility.

As a minister, I have now encountered the limits of that possibility, repeatedly, especially when it comes to worship—the time when most of our people are gathered together. As a queer Black woman responsible for holding open the space for worship and co-creating the container for it, I have also encountered the *depth and breadth* of the limits of that possibility.

When I am authentically thinking of and looking at any given worship theme or moment through my eyes as a queer Black woman, there are many things I might consider. Most importantly, I can look through the eyes of a queer Black woman and not name the experience I am looking through, or I can look through the eyes of a queer Black woman and name that. Most often I am compelled to do the latter, quite intentionally and unapologetically because I know within the depths of my being that my experience and the experiences of others at the margins in our congregations need to be named and heard.

I explicitly name that Black lives matter. I explore America's Constitution, the genocide of Indigenous people, and the enslavement of Black people and its outcomes for everyone residing on these lands. I co-create jazz vespers, collaborating with the Jazz Studies department of Durham's HBCU, or I invite in African dancers and drummers or a multiracial dance company to tell the history of the Civil Rights movement in our Southern city. We celebrate Juneteenth, and bring together a multiracial, multifaith worship team to create a service celebrating Pride in September, when we can proclaim it loud down here in the

South because June is too hot and the students who swell our city during the rest of the year have already gone home by then. I invite descendants of the Saponi to co-create a sacred container with their chants, drums, and stories of how their lands are desecrated today in North Carolina as a result of environmental injustices. We celebrate Kwanzaa each year because Black folk in our congregation want to call in the ancestors, name the nguzo saba (seven principles), share their stories, and light the candles. I am always holding an open-hearted welcome for those who want to co-create worship with meaning making that brings the marginalized to the center.

We take care to create our worship so that it is not exclusively for the marginalized or voyeuristic for the majority, but rather an opportunity for all to open their hearts in ways they had not considered and to experience the fullness of who we in Beloved Community have now become. Ultimately, I believe it is important that the white people in our congregations do not sit back in comfort as though they are not a part of these services or experiences. What weighs upon my heart and the hearts of other marginalized folks in our congregations needs to weigh upon the hearts of all in our community.

And when I do not explicitly name my queer Black womanness but simply lift up my lived experiences of being human, the stories I share about my children, parents, grandparents, or certain friends, are stories steeped in the experiences of being Black in America—even when I am talking about my relationships with friends who are non-Black.

My Blackness is politicized when I show up authentically, whether I want it to be or not. Unless I am intentionally centering whiteness, the experiences of joy, pain, anguish, delight, and hope that are present in my stories are seen as somehow exclusive to me.

Quite frankly, white colleagues approach worship in this same way of bringing their authentic selves to the sacred container all the time, creating liturgy, celebrations, and sermons steeped in personal stories, references, and ideas framed by white dominant culture, which goes unnoticed and certainly unquestioned. Questioning this is like asking fish, "How's the water?" and getting the response, "What water?" But when you are not a part of the dominant culture and you are listening to people present certain experiences, readings, stories, music, and references by and about white, Eurocentric poets and writers, musicians, scientists, researchers, and essayists, you can't help but feel little vexed when folks start getting prickly or uncomfortable about shifting the margins to the center for less than half the year.

It suddenly occurred to me one day that, frankly, even I was hard pressed to come up with a broad variety of sources from Black people, Indigenous people, Latinx, Asian and other people of color on any given topic under the sun. I thought about how worship arts had been taught to me in seminary and wondered about the colonization of my mind, or whether I was simply being lazy-minded. Was I, too, implicitly relegating BIPOC folks to the margins because I was unable to affirm with sure knowledge, grace, and ease that we had something of substance to offer?

I offered myself a challenge: what would it be like for me to spend a year bringing forward sources, whether scientific, philosophical, theological, poetical, musical, or otherwise, that were created solely by Black people, Indigenous people, and all other people of color?

I brought my plan to colleagues I co-created worship with in the congregation at the time, hoping that they too would see an opportunity to be enriched by such a compelling challenge to refine and enrich our offerings to the congregation. They did not, or at least they were not willing to make as radical an effort as I was suggesting. I mentioned this to friends beyond my congregation who were colleagues (of all races and backgrounds) and was surprised by how many expressed worry. Both colleagues I worked with and those who were friends expressed worry that sounded like fear that I'd be leaving people out. *Which people?* I wondered, thinking about the rich scholarship, wisdom, cultures, and communities of Black people, Indigenous people, Latinx, Asian and other people of color the world over.

Suddenly I realized that what people "heard" me say as a Black woman was "Black people," and somehow this felt to them like I was going to be leaving everyone else out. I reminded folks that what I *actually* said was people of color, and that since Black people, Indigenous people, and people of color are the majority in this world, the opposite could reasonably be argued: that no one would be left out, but perhaps we would indeed have fewer white sources if we were really being equitable as we co-created worship.

These are all choices I/we risk making as we co-create worship in our congregations. The inherent risk for me is in the possibility that if or when the gathered community snaps back like a rubber band to its most preferred cultural shape for a sacred container, I will be deemed unneeded as one called to hold it open. But I take on the risk, in the awareness that mine has been a life lived in possibility—and sometimes in impossibility—since well before I became a UU minister. The greater risk is in all that our congregations stand to lose in growth of understanding, compassion, faith, and in fully claiming who they say they want to be in the world.

The irony is that I most love to work collaboratively and creatively with all in building and holding open the sacred container for worship, whether it's for a Sunday morning or whenever and however it might be needed—live or virtual. I hold a deep personal theology that embraces unity rather than separation, though I do acknowledge and support the need for time together among kinfolk, for processing, for self and community care, and for respite among those feeling pressed and oppressed.

But co-creation by all of us of the sacred container that is worship space—sometimes moving forward, sometimes pulling back, in creatively generous, effortless motion—is the worship my heart imagines is possible and what I am always determined to bring forward.

Liberating Pollyanna

SONYA TINSLEY-HOOK

COMMISSIONED 2018*

I am a Pollyanna. I like being happy. I like feeling joy. I really *love* love. Although I don't always succeed, I try to see the positive, the hidden gift, the reason to smile, in almost every situation. As Pollyanna would say, I try to find "reasons to be glad." Now I know what some of you are thinking. How . . . sweet. How quaint. How naïve. And . . . let's be honest . . . *how annoying.*

The fact that calling someone Pollyanna is an insult shows how little we understand the strength and energy that comes from being glad . . . and the transformative power of Joy. I know from my studies of positive psychology and from studying the "book of my own life," that joy is one of the most practical and effective tools that one can use to survive and thrive. Joy is a guiding principle for me and why my daughter's name is Sophia (which means wisdom) *Joi.*

I find that most of the people who ridicule the concept of being a "Pollyanna" have never actually read the book entitled *Pollyanna.* Before he dies and leaves her as a penniless orphan, Pollyanna's kind-hearted

* Because Unitarian Universalism recognizes the priesthood and prophethood of all believers, avenues exist to support the many talented and committed lay members toward alternative paths to ministry. The Central East Region is one of the UUA regions that offers a Commissioned Lay Ministry (CLM) Program. The program develops individualized training in many areas of ministry. Most CLMs serve in their home congregation, but some serve in related venues such as a partner congregation or congregational cluster. Their inclusion in this anthology reflects a commitment to educate Unitarian Universalists about the various ways that ordained ministry and laity interface to strengthen Unitarian Universalism.

father teaches her to find comfort by playing what they call the "glad game." Consequently, when Pollyanna receives only a pair of old crutches in a charity box instead of a doll or anything delightful for Christmas, she and her father decide to find joy in the fact that she has strong legs and doesn't need the crutches! Pollyanna's life is full of challenge and sorrow, yet again and again she finds her strength and renews her energy through finding reasons to be glad despite her hardship. Pollyanna prides herself on being able to creatively find reasons to be glad in even the toughest circumstances. Her tenacious commitment to gladness inspires and motivates the people around her to try and do the same when facing their own struggles. When Pollyanna finally finds herself in a tragic situation that leaves her feeling too defeated and hopeless to play her Glad Game anymore, many of the people she has previously inspired come and help her to slowly and patiently find her way back to strength and joy. They help her to remember how to play the Glad Game again. When I read *Pollyanna*, rather than seeing her Glad Game as something to ridicule, I recognize within it the same strategy that determined Black women have been using for generations to transform disheartening experiences for themselves and their loved ones . . . even if we never called it a game.

Like Pollyanna, I learned to be glad as means of coping with hardship. I wasn't orphaned like Pollyanna. I wasn't sent away to live with a humorless, old aunt. Nor did I ever receive someone else's old crutches for Christmas when what I really wanted was a doll. But I did have to learn how to live with losing my father to cancer when I was only six. I did learn how to help my mother find and roll all the loose change in the house sometimes in order to have enough grocery or gas money until her next paycheck. Aware of how my widowed single mom worked part-time at Wal-Mart in addition to her full-time job just to make ends meet, I learned how to secretly skip lunch and then discreetly manage my growling stomach during the school day in order to use my lunch money for other things like a coveted book by Alice Walker or an album by, I can admit it, Duran Duran! In a world in which Black girls and women are so often disrespected, ridiculed, or just plain ignored, I somehow learned to believe in my own intelligence, creativity, and significance in spite of a world that so often told me otherwise. And just as importantly, I learned to stay in touch, or to at least make a sincere effort to stay in touch, with my joy.

Channeling the spirit and words of the legendary civil rights leader and icon Fannie Lou Hamer when she said she was "sick and tired of being sick and tired," it makes me angry that there are still so many valid reasons in our society for Black women to be angry almost all the time. Therefore I resist as often as I can. Please don't get me wrong. I believe in the necessary and transformative power of anger. But too much anger depletes me and leaves me feeling like escaping from this world rather than working to change it. Too much anger and I find myself losing hope and burning bridges instead of building them. As our sister Audre Lorde eternally reminds us, "The sharing of joy, whether physical, emotional, psychic, or intellectual, forms a bridge between the sharers which can be the basis for understanding much of what is not shared between them, and lessens the threat of their difference." Joy is not the complete answer, but it is an essential piece of the solution. So as often as I am able, I look for ways to be powered and empowered by joy.

I believe in the necessary and transformative power of anger. But too much anger depletes me and leaves me feeling like escaping from this world rather than working to change it.

I believe there are two kinds of joy in life, and perhaps it is not understanding the difference that causes many of us to underestimate joy and deep gladness as sources of strength . . . and as forms of resistance against all that seeks to devalue, displace, and deny us. I think of these two kinds of joy as *wildflower joy* and *homegrown joy*. Wildflower joy is what many of us think of as the only kind of joy. It's the emotion that springs up during our happiest moments, making us feel that for a brief time, all is right with the world. Wildflower joy comes and goes in our lives. It's such a beautiful feeling, but you can't count on it to remain and you never know when and where you will find it.

Homegrown joy is the joy that we must plant and cultivate ourselves or else there won't be any. It can live indefinitely, but it must be consistently watered, staked, protected from frost, pruned, repotted, harvested for seeds—nurtured and kept alive. It's the decision we make to remember what is still good when so much has been lost. It is fertilized with gratitude for what is still there to sustain and strengthen us. It's a mindset that helps us to remember that things could easily be worse and, in fact, always are worse today, right now, for someone. You find it in these words of the old African American gospel favorite immortalized by Mahalia Jackson, "How I got over, how I got over, you know my soul looks back in wonder at how I got over. . . ."

Homegrown joy strengthens us. It is what Black women are thinking about when we remind each other not to let some negative person or circumstance "steal our joy," which I believe is our own culturally relevant version of Pollyanna's Glad Game. Homegrown joy is the only kind that is effective as an act of resistance because even though we can let it go, no one else can ever really take it or steal it from us. Yet it also moves us beyond just resistance to, in the words of Alice Walker, starting to "live in the world today as you wish everyone to live in the world to come."

I think homegrown joy is the kind that the African American writer and activist Brittany Packnett Cunningham is referring to when she writes, "Joy is a break from a news cycle that will discombobulate me if I let it. Joy is a middle finger to a bigot with a torch who wants to see me cower." For those of us who believe that we have meaningful and urgent work to do in order to help transform our world into one that is more peaceful, just, and loving, there is simply not enough time or space for too much cynicism and despair. We must grow and distribute as much of our strength-giving, hope-building, fortifying homegrown joy as we are able—and we must do it today. Yesterday would not be too soon because the presence of joy is essential to every positive change we want to make possible in this world.

On some level, all people, regardless of whether they are Unitarian Universalists, want to have more joy in their lives. What I hope distinguishes those of us who identify as UU is what we choose to do with our hard-won homegrown joy when we are really living out our values and Principles. My hope is that we listen and learn with intention from the multitudes of Black women who, through the years and through seemingly insurmountable circumstances, have refused to let anyone steal their joy. My hope is that we use our own joy to create a world in which well-being, purpose, abundance, community, and justice are possible for each one of us, no matter who we are or how we have been marginalized and unvalued. Our challenge as well as our charge is to live openly and hopefully as more conscious and evolved Pollyannas, working together to build a world in which absolutely everyone can experience an abundance of reasons for which they can truly be glad.

May it be so. And may we help and be helped in making it so.

Root to Rise

REV. YADENEE HAILU
PRELIMINARY FELLOWSHIP 2019

I was called right out of my comfort zone in the fall of 2014. I had only been introduced to Unitarian Universalism two months prior when I found myself, in the church garden, feeling a call to ministry.

The journey of discernment was/is often lonesome. People shared, "Seminary challenged my faith." I wish I was warned of what I found instead, that seminary challenged my faith in humanity ... and frankly my desire to partner with it.

> *The journey of discernment was/is often lonesome. People shared, "Seminary challenged my faith." I wish I was warned of what I found instead, that seminary challenged my faith in humanity ... and frankly my desire to partner with it.*

When well-intentioned peers remark, "Papers are the hardest part," I wish I could yell back to myself, "Girl, seminary isn't the hard part! Empire is. And Empire is loud and strong in the myriad of institutions you will learn, intern, and work in. It's in the assignments, discussions, and grading. It's in the program, internship, credentialing process, and jobs. At times you will feel well near drowned and wonder, *Am I subjecting myself to torture for love? Why in the hell am I here going through this?!*

I can't yell back to myself, but I can reflect on what sustained, fortified, and continues to propel me in ministry and beyond. It sort of started with my decision to like nature.

Every year I like to have an intuited focus, and my first year of seminary was supposed to be "the year of camping." This grand title was backed by zero camping, fire building, outdoor hiking, or wilderness experience. I was a nature newbie, and I wanted to close the gap between us. I borrowed a tent, sleeping bag, and flashlight; located a nearby campsite; loaded up my car; and set out.

When I was a kid, I was known to quickly run back indoors after seeing too many birds fly overhead, feeling an ant crawling up my leg, or hearing the neighbor's dog bark too loudly. Once back in my safe space, I often told my mom matter-of-factly while still catching my breath, "I'm a nature girl, Mom. I love being in nature! . . . Just not yet . . . I will when I'm older."

Well, I was older, in grad school, and felt the call. This was the year of camping! Thus into nature I went to face foreign plants, uncontrolled weather, creepy crawlies, even creepier sounds, and the imminent threat of being non-consensually touched by an animal or a bug. There were a few obstacles but I knew, deep down, "I love being in nature." And whatever a "nature girl" was, damn it, I was it!

I remember my first camping trip in fragments. It was hazy at best due to a few less-than-ideal circumstances. The weekend was hot and humid at 97 degrees Fahrenheit. Unfortunately, I didn't think to pitch my borrowed tent in the shade or bring a chair, food, or enough water. Additionally, I was swirling with nerves, the impulse to run back indoors, and the determination to return to my destined love of nature. Due to the stressors, I still don't recall many highlights from that first camping trip—except for the vivid memory of driving away from that campground the next day, shimmering with delight and confidence. Let me explain.

I started the trip with a three-mile hike that took four hours longer than it should have because I went rogue and got very, very lost. Then I discovered back at the car that the water bottle consumed on the hike was all that I had thought to pack. Sure, it was good luck I had one package of air fried green beans in my glove compartment to ration a post hike-snack, dinner, breakfast, and lunch. And, yes, it's to be expected that I failed after two hours to build a fire when I was armed with only matches and a receipt for kindling. I woke up stiff, sweaty, and sore. The extended hike and night spent on the ground in a sleeping bag designed for below-freezing temperatures rather than sticky hot Oklahoma summers cemented my muscles and joints. Unfortunately, the tent also trapped heat. I staggered outside early in the morning to the sun already beating down. I found a makeshift seat on a rock and looked at my meagre campsite. I was hungry, thirsty, sweating, and stressed. *What. On. Earth. Am. I. Doing. Out. Here!?* I wondered. *What are campers supposed to do? Should I just leave early?"* Y'all, I was tired, uncomfortable, kind of bored, and consistently scared.

I don't know where the time went for the rest of that morning. I probably watched what I could. Touched what felt safe. And listened to the space around me moving at the humble pace of my tender body. I was out there for five or six more hours until I packed up and finally sat in my car at noon. My body temperature was at last cooling with shade and air conditioning.

What's up? I asked my body and felt back, *I am alive!* I was hungry, thirsty, and sore, but I also felt immense relief and strength. I felt pride and determination to do it again, even better. I faced nature and was starting to get to know her, and she was teaching me about myself and my power. A love was rekindling. The earth and I had some catching up to do, and I vowed to learn, adapt, and have fun while getting close.

On my second solo camping trip, with more borrowed gear, I upped the ante. I brought water, food, a lawn chair, and a lighter. I also pitched my tent under a tree, chose a cooler weekend, and even scored a water view. I didn't get a fire started, but I wasn't overheated, hungry, or thirsty!

I didn't immediately master everything, but I had noticeably improved by studying, learning, integrating, and adapting.

It was on this second camping trip of my "year of camping" that I found myself sitting (in the chair I brought) looking at a tree and wondering, *What am I supposed to do on a camping trip?* I was genuinely hoping for an answer. I sat and waited. My mind wandered and settled. I noticed and followed sensations. Then an idea floated past my mind. It felt like a dance or joke. I needed to write it down to inspect it more closely.

Soon I was rummaging through my tent, bag, and car to find a pen and paper. (I didn't pack any. "Of course." I laughed. "Okay, noted for next time.") I retrieved my phone from the car, and began tethering the inspiration to my screen with words and rhythm. (See "where is leaf" on page 197.)

I felt electric as the dancing in my mind became words I could enjoy by another medium. Here, immersed with the natural world, a love letter laced in theology tumbled out. At the intersection of chirping birds and a glistening lake where I sat under a tree, fresh with the satisfaction of doing what I can to feel safe, curious, and open, I became ecstatically aware of Love pulsing between every atom of matter. At least that's what I felt in my gut while I reread the poem. There is more Love than matter, the swell of wonder concluded in my heart. Life force can be known in so very many ways but it's in the experiencing that it is known and in the knowing that it is loved.

All this the carbon-built earth could infinitely remind my carbon-built body. Returning to its aliveness, when I willingly experience Life, nature, and get to know it. This remembering of Life takes sprout in my mind, body, and heart, blooming a healing elixir (Love) for that which aches. Pouring personalized concoctions of contentment, wellness, hope, vitality, excitement, rest, protection, innovation, and more. Life returning to Life is the vessel and fragrance of Love. This is *salvation, awakening, healing,* or any other name put to the mercy of life returning to Life by way of Love.

Throughout my life, nature has been my greatest teacher, healer, and friend. In fact, the Network of Life has been my doula and touchstone in the chaotic change and heartbreak of ministry. When I've been gutted by empire, unchecked in colleagues and institutions, stunned by stinginess, tormented by trauma, or just too tired to even—I return to my beloved and am soothed. Not "fixed up" so I can get right back to it, but returned to Life, often with a new framework, showered in grace and drenched in Love.

The trees I sit with don't ask what my credentials are; they ask if I am well. The brook giggling while I dip my feet in it doesn't remind me to answer emails, but to get free. Leaves have taught me the art of change and compost. The ocean has recalibrated my nervous system for free. And the moon continues to remind me of the gentle parts in me no matter the weariness I endure.

I think the absolutely hardest parts of empire in ministry are what fool us into centering empty things—buildings over people and plants, reputation over relationships. We break our own hearts when ministry becomes synonymous with busy. When we trade our voice to privilege academia and a grade. When we are enslaved to committees and traditions, forgetting that empty things such as these are meant to serve Life rather than the other way around. We drain our energy and weaken ourselves and our communities by putting up obstacles to life returning to Life. When we break from nature's way, by hoarding instead of relearning rhythm and redistribution, or use survival to fuel our days instead of rest and ease, we are centering empty things and we pay the price with our life force.

I know for sure that life centers Life. Nature doesn't isolate success to the growth and preservation stages of life. It gracefully embodies every season, including rest and the transformation of life vessels (death and compost). Life centers Life. It trusts intuition and respects bodies. Life's fruits are mutuality, movement, and medicine.

By studying the carbon around and in me, I've remembered how to heal. I am loyal first and foremost to the Network of Life, the force that can be known in infinite ways. As it is experienced, the Network of Life evokes Love. I am loyal to Life organizing for Life. And that is my ministry, a love of life returning to Life because its fruits are healing, integration, and wholeness.

I don't know what I'll get around to being or doing, what my titles will be, or if I will have any. But I trust that I'll be cultivating a regenerative ecosystem around, in, and through me to heal, to love, and to center Life.

Self Becoming Light

MELISSA C. JETER
COMMISSIONED 2019*

To live and yet feel invisible to the world is a great violent act to the soul. To be seen and to be betrayed by the group to whom you have shared your light is a brutal blow. For what reason is there to diminish the light in the womb where the self is becoming? Who goes against the generative act of shining the light?

During the 2016 presidential campaign, I watched Rev. Dr. William J. Barber of the New Poor People's Campaign on Facebook speak at the Unitarian Universalist Cleveland Society. I could no longer let my growing sense of self be hidden under a bushel by systems of oppression, privilege, misogyny, and racism. Barber talked simply about interlocking systems of oppression to a broadly diverse group of people. I had turned away from media debates about who might be the next president of the United States. Rev. Barber sparked hope in my heart that I might find a moral and mature faith in Unitarian Universalism. I wanted white

---

* Because Unitarian Universalism recognizes the priesthood and prophethood of all believers, avenues exist to support the many talented and committed lay members toward alternative paths to ministry. The Central East Region is one of the UUA regions that offers a Commissioned Lay Ministry (CLM) Program. The program develops individualized training in many areas of ministry. Most CLMs serve in their home congregation, but some serve in related venues such as a partner congregation or congregational cluster. Their inclusion in this anthology reflects a commitment to educate Unitarian Universalists about the various ways that ordained ministry and laity interface to strengthen Unitarian Universalism.

Melissa C. Jeter is now in seminary at Methodist Theological School in Ohio and a student minister at the First Unitarian Church of Toledo.

folks in my church to, at the very least, use the privilege they had to side with the poor, the stranger, and those considered "the least of these." I felt free to listen to the inner nagging voice that called me to become a brighter burning light.

Voice Is Vocation

My voice called me to write about faithful and universal principles and the need for justice, as I had done when I first started community work. This time, I wrote from my direct experience with gardening on my blog, *Hip Urban Farmer*. Every blog entry was about more than growing food. The voice coming through described a vision of the future based on the potential in a small black-eyed pea seed. I could look at the black-eyed pea seed and envision pods being shucked and peas simmering in a pot with smoked turkey. Even though I had not accomplished my personal goal to be an urban farmer, I had embraced this complex vision through writing, and it became fertile ground for the cultivation of a moral and mature faith that recognized that reaping is directly related to sowing. I could see that in each and every moment, we can all have long-term effects on dismantling oppression, if we could just focus our attention on what we could do. My heart called me to write from my direct experiences over years of studying and practicing community work. The calling in my soul was much like an echo in a valley among the hills at the tip of urban Appalachia where I was born.

I was raised by a father with a Baptist religious background and a mother who attended a Pentecostal church established by her family in small southeastern Ohio. To my young mind, belonging to the family Pentecostal faith meant that all I had to do was accept the creed and doctrine. Yet according to the Bible my family used, this perception is contradicted in James 2:14-17:

What does it profit, my brethren, if someone says he has faith but does not have works? Can faith save him? If a brother or sister is naked and destitute of daily food, and one of you says to them, "Depart in peace, be warmed and filled," but you do not give them the things which are needed for the body, what does it profit? Thus also faith by itself, if it does not have works, is dead.

I focused my attention on the life-sustaining service of my maternal grandmother, who called people into greater community by counseling them, often on the phone. In one instance, my grandmother had a young pregnant girl staying with her just after my grandmother's return home from the hospital. The girl lived with my grandmother under the auspices of caring for my grandmother. While a heart attack brought my grandmother to the hospital, I cannot understand how her heart was broken. She served love to everyone as far as I could tell.

Soul Resonance

Shame proved to be an obstacle in my development. My early childhood experiences with church were the opposite of compassionate. My grandmother's insistence that I and my brother attend church was reinforced by my mother's physical coercion. My father did not attend church at all. It did not escape my attention that the man of the house, to whom I deferred for most of my information and learning, stayed home watching football. I was quiet in Sunday school because I was uncertain about God. I felt that I would be considered bad if I expressed any of my feelings. I did not know if God existed or not. I once heard my mother complain that my father did not believe anymore. To stay safe from the judgment of Sunday school teachers, relatives, and my mother, I thought it would be best to observe and listen.

I was emotionally disconnected from my relatives at our Pentecostal church in the city. I knew little about them, as I lived apart from most of my city-dwelling relatives in a nearby small town. I was reserved at church, in contrast to the shouting and speaking in tongues happening in the pews all around me. I just listened to the rhythm of the preacher and anticipated the choir with great joy. I loved the singing at church. Even though I sang everywhere outside of church, my mother told me I could not sing. I was also not "saved," so I sometimes still wonder if that was the true reason for my exclusion from singing in church. I have little recollection of being asked or encouraged to participate in church functions, unless it was to recite a Bible verse in front of the congregation during a major holiday. It is still a mystery to me why I was told that I could not sing.

In my late twenties, I was interested in actively doing justice work. I know now that it was a call to ministry, but I didn't quite understand the call. I had just graduated from the University of Toledo with a Master of Arts in sociology, specializing in theories of community organizing and community development. I was drawn to study womanist theology as a consequence of my graduate studies focus on the intersection of race, sex, gender, and class.

I was still trying to find my religious path. My moral compass directed me to do justice seeking work. I yearned to be intentional about building justice in community. These words by adrienne maree brown, Black feminist and author, affirmed my understanding then and now of the light that I wanted to be: "Without intention, we are usually practicing what the dominant society wants us to practice—competing with each other to be cogs in a system that benefits the owning class, vaguely religious, vaguely patriotic."

From 1995 through 2004, I worked many jobs, often three at a time. Some were clearly influential in my faith development. For example, I worked for a community development corporation. I surveyed folks door-to-door in an urban neighborhood to find out how the nonprofit I worked for could help revitalize the community. I gladly walked through the resource-starved neighborhood. I worked with folks on clean-ups. It was good, inspiring work. I had another job as a research assistant. This afforded me the opportunity to attend a popular education seminar on participatory research at the Highlander Research and Education Center. Besides my community work, I spent a lot of time as adjunct faculty teaching sociology in community colleges. But I never really felt satisfied. The work was hard. It was emotionally and physically exhausting, and it did not pay well. I was also bewildered by both community workers' and community organizations' lack of compassion in their work with marginalized peoples seeking justice. I started to realize that there was a huge gap between working for justice and actually achieving it. I was burnt out. Luckily for me, in the midst of all of this, I found Unitarian Universalism in 1999.

A friend who was developing community computing centers and working in her neighborhood association suggested that I might like her local Unitarian Universalist church. When I read the seven Principles and saw the possibility of justice work within Unitarian Universalism, I was excited to attend. I recall feeling odd that I was in a church where most of the people were white. However, there were people who liked knitting and needlework as much as I did. I found people with whom I could connect. Still, it was not easy to switch between working in a poor Black urban neighborhood and worshipping in a predominantly white middle class church. It was not easy to overcome the shame that I might just be going to hell as my mother's religion preached, regardless of the fact that I did not believe in hell or a white father figure god.

I became a regular member of the young adult group, and later I taught religious education for senior high students. I wanted my high school mentor to visit church with me. She lived in Michigan and sent "Happy Black History Month" cards to me every February. I wanted to know what she thought about this church and Unitarian Universalism.

I invited her in February 2002, and she was much impressed with the service and readings. I also noted that she had made a great impression on the minister. Having noted that my mentor and minister had met with mutual respect, I began to release some of the religious shame and embrace Unitarian Universalism as my faith.

Generativity

It was during this time that the minister hired a local gospel music director to teach a small group to sing gospel music. I happened to be at church when the gospel choir was just getting started in the sanctuary. I never had the opportunity to even consider the choir of my Pentecostal youth. I was irreverently apathetic about being the only African American among white folks singing Black gospel music. I decided to stay and sing.

Everything the gospel director taught filled the gaps of a Black experience that I was missing. The small gospel choir, with an African American female director, in this Unitarian Universalist church was a small, generative, dark space where I was becoming a bright light. Still, I had some discomfort with the humanist theology and classical music sensibilities of church members, including our regular choir director.

The gospel choir soon died, but not the flame burning in me and some of the other gospel choir members. So we joined a community gospel choir directed by the same woman. I continued to sing in church. Shyly, quietly, I sang contemporary folk songs about the need for justice in the world. The minister told me that she thought I had a calling for the ministry, but that I shouldn't worry about it. Meanwhile, though my spouse encouraged my singing activities, he told me that he would leave me if I became an evangelical minister. He was as adamant about leaving if I became a minister as he was in favor of my singing. It was a double bind for me.

In 2004, I was laid off and burnt out from seeing people lose their homes through predatory lending practices. It was not illegal to sell a nearly uninhabitable house to a person who had little if any income or knowledge about personal finance and the upkeep of a home. It was not illegal to attach balloon payments to mortgage contracts after three to five years of regular payments. It was not illegal to buy and sell mortgages in securities. It was not illegal, but it was not right to cause people to endure so much pain. I wanted to give voice to what I saw.

Once again, I heard the call to ministry. I sought counseling from another minister who advised me to get into a graduate writing program, if I wanted to write about what I saw. I was freelancing in non-profit organizations and underemployed while my spouse worked full time. My spouse had applied for a job in Boston. I thought that maybe this was my chance to pursue another graduate program, so I took the opportunity to visit Harvard University. I attended the orientation for the divinity school while he had his interview.

Unfortunately, the job in Boston did not come to fruition. I thought about the type of work that Black women usually did in the existing economy. I read about changes to come in the economy and where those places might be in the city where I lived. Consequently, I chose to attend the Harvard of library schools, the University of Illinois at Urbana-Champaign. In 2007, I obtained a job as a librarian in the public library. A year later, I completed my degree and I ended my marriage. Once again, I started to sing in church. Our current minister started a worship associate program. I joined the program, and she became my mentor. I initially modeled my role as a worship associate on the commissioned lay leader who worked with the minister. Though he did not mentor me in my role, I was careful to observe and learn from him. I made my own choices about how I would be a worship associate with the guidance of the minister. The minister recommended that I attend the summer camp for Unitarian Universalists in the Central

East Region. I applied for a scholarship and attended my first summer camp in 2011.

There was some kind of magic to being once again irreverently apathetic about being one of a handful of Black faces at the camp. I jumped right into the choir and into singing. I became fast friends with folks in my dorm, particularly a lesbian couple on my floor. They hatched a plan to create a small band with me as the lead singer. We played in the small ensembles at the end of the week.

Over the years, this band of folks would be instrumental in my growth as a singer and a minister. I can say that in preceding years, I had experienced some lonely times at camp as a regular attendee. Although I was meeting new people and we shared the same faith, we knew very little about each other. I was uncomfortable. There were people who confused me and my name with another African American woman who was there. There were people who I suspect were scared to reach out to me, but I continued to build relationships and sow seeds in our faith tradition of Unitarian Universalism. I think people were afraid to take the risk to befriend someone they did not know. In addition, there were people who were very reserved and found it uncomfortable to reach out. Moreover, Unitarian Universalism has had cultural roots that discourage people from connecting to each other by talking about their faith. The good news of community and connection and affirmation of a responsible search for truth and meaning draws people to Unitarian Universalism, but most Unitarian Universalists identify as white and there was and still is a good degree of social distance between white and non-white people in American society in general. Our congregations have few intercultural relationships.

I addressed my stress and discomfort by digging in and extending my roots in this faith. I read books about African American Unitarian Universalists and the faith. Also, I sang. I sang from the depths of the pain in my soul, intent on making people feel every vibration, every note, and every word. Eventually, I had to learn how to respond to the compliments and later invitations to sing with people. If this was a problem, then it was a good one to have. I continued to extend my roots in Unitarian Universalism despite my discomfort. I used the discomfort as fertilizer for my own growth. I could put all the discomfort and pain into a song. I created a role for myself with my voice and it affected people. A singer asked me to join the camp's planning committee. This call to service inspired me. Yet, there were also a teacher and nearly a dozen ministers who added fuel, igniting the growing and burning flame of my faith during this time.

I remain Unitarian Universalist because I desire a moral and mature faith to guide my life. I also need a community where I can feel free to search, grow, and change without pressure to stay the same. The more involved I become in Unitarian Universalism, the brighter I grow and the happier I am.

In the Spring of 2016, I completed the paperwork to enter the Commissioned Lay Ministry Program of the Central East Region of the Unitarian Universalist Association. During my enrollment, I was paired with a mentoring minister. I also read and studied from a required reading list. The program consisted of three years of reading, preaching, social justice ministry, and—of course—singing.

On March 31, 2019, I was commissioned as a lay minister in my church through the Central East Region of the Unitarian Universalist Association. Unitarian Universalism focuses on making the world a kinder and more loving place. I intend to lend my voice to that goal, because I want to live in a world that is kind, loving, and compassionate. Some twenty years later, my desire to be an instrument for justice and compassion is most important to me. My empathy drives me to action. I want to do what I can to ease pain and suffering.

I remain Unitarian Universalist because I desire a moral and mature faith to guide my life. I also need a community where I can feel free to search, grow, and change without pressure to stay the same. The more involved I become in Unitarian Universalism, the brighter I grow and the happier I am. The call to ministry has been a journey in and of itself. Much like in music rooted in African American tradition, there were many calls and many responses. Each call and response sowed seeds for the harvest of faith I am reaping now. I am still becoming a light in the world. And I am letting that light shine brightly.

POETRY

Meditation to Ministers

REV. TONI VINCENT

Spirit of hope and of our highest and finest selves, your presence brings brightness to our eyes and gives us courage when our own efforts fail. Be close through the tunnels and the tangles of our fears; keep us reminded that our strength is in one another. African American ministers have gathered together in this city to find ourselves and to remember who we are—our ministry of justice, a tireless task in a world of suffering and hurt. Protect us from the hazards of our charge, the weariness of repeated battles, the indifference of power to pain, the strength of our foes, the seductions that would have us abandon the struggle for worldly goods and comforts. Remain with us a dearest friend, for you, and with you; we aspire to more than is reasonable, more than our limitations would suggest. We hope, we offer hope, we bring hope to the face of cruel oppressions, and there the battle lines are drawn. Amen.

Spirit of the Moment

REV. TONI VINCENT

Here in this holy place, on this day of fading Summer and
beckoning Fall, let us give ourselves to the Spirit of the
moment and find the Sacred Oneness that binds all life
together.
Knowing that much is beyond our ability to change, life
calls us still to act in compassion and fairness wherever the
opportunity presents itself.
Let us seize the strength of the ritual, remember, renew,
and relive the taste of hard-fought struggles in the human
search for justice.
We are hungry for the lessons of the past and for guidance
toward the promise of the future. May we be open to
all that expands our awareness, and welcome all to enter our
embrace. Amen.

Jazz Vespers

REV. JACQUELINE BRETT

Life is veiled and hidden,
even as your greater self is
hidden and veiled.
Yet when life speaks, all the winds become words;
and when she speaks again,
the smiles upon your lips
and the tears in your eyes
turn also into words.
When she sings, the deaf hear and are held;
and when she comes walking
the sightless behold her
and are amazed
and follow her in wonder and astonishment.

Thus wrote
LebaneseAmerican poet Khalil Gibran.

What I know for sure is that when
Life
deigns to be embodied

This poem was originally co-created as a homily for a jazz vespers service
with musicians from the Jazz Studies Department of North Carolina Central
University.

in the becoming
and becoming
and becoming
of each one of us,
it is only then that she is *truly* something to behold.
The awesome beauty and magnificent terror,
the fierce strength and tender fragility of
Life
embodied as human being human
in all its glorious and terrible forms:
each one of us
bursting
into being out of the DNA of stars
now cells and sinews and bone and blood and flesh.
Life
now speaking in the high-pitched wail
of we newly arrived and baby born
into human consciousness and
whatever
Life wants to offer us
into
whatever
we choose to offer it.
And so the seasons begin.

But about that baby:
the greatest story ever told me about a
newborn babe was . . . .
——— no, not that one,

but this one———
by a spiritual teacher
in full awareness of her manifestation
as Divine Feminine
in the flesh,
who said the greatest gift she had ever been given
was by her mother——— yes, her
real
live
earth mother, —
who was never deluded by the pudgy cuteness
and smallness of her child
but always treated her as
a being
in
full
conscious
awareness
of herself.

The only allowance her mother made
was that her daughter was yet
small
and had not yet grown into the full stature
of her human body,
and also she could not yet speak
in a language her mother
understood———but she knew that would come———
because

express herself
her daughter could,
and her mother knew that if
she as Mother truly listened,
"time bending stretching . . .
listened for maybe hours or minutes"
her daughter would be understood and,
if given the space
to consciously co-create her world,
her daughter would.

And so she did.
And so she does.

The extraordinariness of this story for me
is that it is made of
Black
Girl
Magic
a little Black Girl
made aware that
she
Is
over three quarters of a century ago
when an unconscious world
told her day after day after day,
season after season,
that she
is
not.

I am awed by the great gift in this
for any of us
and have often wondered what it
might mean to treat a child,
any child,
in that very first season of life
as one
whose greater Self
lies not
hidden and veiled
but is recognized and revealed
to oneself:

the great
I Am That I Am
Self
as Spirit of Life in the physical
fat body thin body
small body giant body
black body brown body
pink body white body
he body she body
they body them body.
We bodies.
Earth bodies.

Fully aware
that
We have all come,

now what shall We consciously co-create
together
with All That Is
in All This Awesomeness?
Note that I did not say accomplish,
but co-create,
out of conscious awareness
of that which lies hidden and veiled,
undeluded
by the illusion
of what we are not
or deeply don't even want to be,
no matter how good it looks on the outside,
because this is no ego trip
when we deeply understand
we are not those things
in the hidden and veiled
spaces of the
greater Essential Self.

And so what might we co-create in full embrace of
this knowing that
we are possibility
    from a sudden burst of light?
That we are the light?

So what might we co-create in the
love power and wisdom of the
I Am Spirit
that is Life?

And even still,

with the knowing that we are in the physical,

that we are in a time space limitation

with bodies that eventually stop working

as we believe they should

and often far sooner than most of us would like,

freak accidents, mutated genes,

chemical imbalances,

cells and hormones that go rogue and betray us

and there but for the grace of . . . .

But we come to appreciate the resilience of our forms,

how they can withstand an onslaught of the harshest toxins

at least for a while

and all the little parts that actually do work, especially the

     parts

we didn't even know we had

but come to understand we do need,

and so we stand in gratitude

and with appreciation.

Because here's the thing:

even in this

we are

the Possibility that is

each one of us

bursting

into being out of the DNA of stars

now cells and sinews and bone and blood and flesh

Life
now living season upon season upon season
hopefully
become awake and aware
in human consciousness and
whatever
Life wants to offer us
into
whatever
we choose to offer it.
And such is the way of the seasons
and our
Selves.

Behold
with wonder and awe.

Where Is Leaf

REV. YADENEE HAILU

Where is leaf now
here in the snow months removed
from her coloring and falling
Where is leaf

Earth speaks
Follow her physical path
Her journey from branch to dirt
There feeding back
seemingly dust there is leaf

What say you then about her chemistry
remarks a lark
Essence was extracted and stored in tree's skeleton
Await spring
There again I know leaf will be

Wind whispers seek leaf through me
in her movement and dance
Final fall from grace
Leaf loved me
Now blows still her sacred soul

I've gathered your knowing and truths
Tangible body, shared biology,
and mystic's beloved
But for most even you
Mystery was revealed in memory

I knew leaf
I felt her, saw her
She was with me and lost to me
Remembrance
There lives leaf

Endlessly
growing, changing, moving, feeding,
cycling through we and more

Is she not God
Is this not God
Are we not God

There

REV. CONNIE SIMON

Feels like we've been traveling forever
but we're still not there. Lord knows we've tried—each in our
own way—to get there,
wherever "there" is.
Working groups, task forces, coalitions, allies. Resolutions
and programs. Catchy acronyms and fancy names. We think
and think and talk and talk. Then think and talk some more.
Lord knows we've tried—each—our own way—to get there,
wherever "there" is.
They try so hard to include me. But I thought I was already
included. Now I feel like an outsider. Lord knows we've
tried—each in our own way—to get there,
wherever "there" is.
I know it's better than it was. But it still feels like I'm
supposed to
set aside a piece of who I am in order to belong. I won't do
it. My Unitarian and Universalist ancestors worked too hard
for me to give up now. Frances Ellen Watkins Harper
whispers softly in my ear, "keep going, child." Yes, ma'am.
It's a struggle sometimes but
I don't feel no ways tired.
We've made some progress and we'll make some more. We'll
keep trying. We'll get there someday. Wherever "there" is.

Black Girl BLUUs

MELISSA C. JETER

I don't want to mourn Black girl blues, though there are
times I really want to be seen
I just really want to do my own thing.
Maybe I'll jump at the sun and smile knowing that
what's in my head and on my heart
is a beautiful work of art.
Sometimes, I get angry and internalize it;
I get real stubborn about what I know I am about,
what I know I have the skills to do.
I smirk when the people say, who knew?
I could be invisible and I thought for a long time that I was
as I was looking out and they were looking upon . . .
What . . . what did they see?
Surely it was not Me; just projections of their imaginings
and
proscriptive roles of enmeshment and co-dependency.
Nah, they never really see me.
Because the eyes they do deceive
and their heart is never near to me
and their mind is so full of scientific designs and
enlightenment.
They know so they are closed to me.
So in many ways I am free,

free when I breathe deeply on my zafu
And face Tina, Black Jesus, the brown naked goddesses, the
triune of scarf-covered brown-shaded women with hands
upturned in prayer, as well as the storyteller figurine on all
fours covered in tiny children from Ecuador;
I am free when I read Susan Taylor, former editor of *Essence
Magazine*—
words that say Let go.
And I breathe out and see that love is truly free.
Just let go.
I straighten my back; my second chakra opens.
I listen and hear, Grow up.
I look at Tina and I hear her say, I don't really want to fight
anymore.
There are all kinds of people in this world.
Some will die for you, some will lie to you . . .
And then I am aurally directed to Ruthie singing Maya,
saying, "Pretty women wonder where my secret lies.
I'm not cute or built to suit a fashion model size
but when I start to tell them they think I'm telling lies."
One more deep breath
and I have centered myself for the
practice that is ineffable connection,
an assertion to That which flows through me
and every living thing.
I know it's true, because that's when the cat cries out.
I really won't mourn, though I sing the blues.
Maya said that my ticket was bought.
My ancestors paid the dues.

Epilogue

REV. DR. ADELE SMITH-PENNIMAN

Threads intertwine in many of these reflections written by Black Unitarian Universalist women in ministry. At first glance, they may seem contradictory, but a closer examination reveals how together they inform so many sisters' journeys. For the first theme, I borrow the title of the late Rev. Marjorie Bowens-Wheatley's narrative, "Not by Ourselves Alone." It is fitting that we call out the names of saints who walked during the early days of Black women entering the ministry, and Bowens-Wheatley is one such shero who embodied strength with grace. Again and again in these pages, contributors name people who enabled them to even consider ministry and who walked beside them when the road became rocky: a grandparent embodying church in the fullest sense; a mentor saying, "I see you"; a DRUUMM (Diverse Revolutionary Unitarian Universalist Multicultural Ministries) or BLUU (Black Lives of Unitarian Universalism) gathering encouraging us to bring our tears and our dreams. One reflection notes the many times the writer thought of leaving behind the UUA but fellow people of color pulled her back from the ledge. Consistently, we wrote of the critical importance of an Amen Corner. Rev. Dr. Rebekah Savage titles her essay "Ubuntu: I Am Because We Are."

I suspect that for many African Americans, family and community—even when fractured—play a significant role in our lives. The second common theme in this anthology is how hard, lonely, and even traumatic being a Black clergywoman can be.

Rev. Yadenee Hailu describes how "seminary challenged my faith in humanity and frankly my desire to partner with it. . . . Empire is loud and strong in the myriad of institutions you will learn, work, and intern in. . . . Why in the hell am I here going through this?" The candidating process can be no less daunting. Irrespective of age and experience, women are steered to associate positions or small churches. Rev. Dr. Michelle Bentley was told she would have to do church starts if she wanted a pulpit. Another, interviewing with a search committee, was chastised by the white senior pastor that, of course, there would be no racism because his was "a very liberal congregation."

Rev. Dr. Kristen Harper reflects on her adoption into a UU family at eighteen months of age. She recounts her experiences as a little brown girl in a sea of white faces, first as a child, then as a lay leader and finally as a minister. She recalls some of the early Black UU clergy women who shaped her ministry and how she evolved to identify as a spiritual humanist.

Rev. Jacqueline Brett's beautiful piece explores the theme of life built around a periodic Saturday jazz vespers that her congregation co-creates with community partners. She ponders the possibility of Black Girl Magic when little brown and Black girls are allowed to live in a world "not hidden and veiled" but "recognized and revealed."

A beloved elder left the UUA. She was called to her family church but the UUA refused to recognize her ministry because the congregation was not "officially" UU and then refrained from supporting a wider search. This is only one of several stories like this that are not included in this anthology. For every story that is told we must understand that there are always more.

Black clergy note how often at UU gatherings white people mix up their names and stories, indicating that too often we are noted for our "race" and not as unique individuals. Repeatedly, writers in this volume fear they are mere tokens and trophies. A seminarian who was interviewed wondered, while rubbing her brown skin, "Do they want *me* or do they want *this?*"

Rev. Addae Ama Kraba's essay tells the story of her five years in parish ministry, marked by roadblocks—beginning with the white congregation believing that, with her hiring, they had completed their work on white privilege and systemic oppressions. They thwarted her leadership. Passive aggressive behavior spread, particularly among male parishioners. Too often when sisters speak up, we are castigated as the problem and dismissed as Angry Black Women. Our community holds stories of African American women forced to prematurely leave a position or else be run out of town. I was attacked for naming the racism breeding in her congregation and the district executive was brought in to reprimand her. Rev. Dr. Qiyamah Rahman called out the problematic behavior of a white male minister and fire rained down on *her* as though she were the one who had trespassed. These are some of the stories Black clergy women share in this anthology.

Divisions within the UUA are marked and the wagons circle when an "outsider" challenges a more powerful colleague. Rev. Dr. Natalie Maxwell Fenimore experienced the treatment of religious educators as second-class citizens by some clergy. Still others point to a hierarchy of parish ministers over community ministers. Furthermore, the trauma some Black ministers experience also atomizes our collegiality. Particularly among elders, some people have had to periodically pull inward to discern and heal. At a recent BLUU symposium, the absence of many trailblazers pointed to the pain too many have experienced. Depression, anxiety, and PTSD are some of the clinical labels caused by our trauma.

Another theme threaded through this collection is the search for spiritual home. Two contributors holding roots in two denominations have lingering questions about UU identity. I, for one, miss the Black presence I experienced in the United Church of Christ and the UCC's more inclusive and less dogmatic theology. Unitarianism Universalism can be parochial when it shies away from beliefs and practices deemed not sufficiently "progressive."

An important theme reflected in this anthology and interlocking with the others is hope and joy. For some, this is expressed in a passion for social justice. We envision a more whole and holy world and commit to work, however incremental our steps, toward its actualization. Rev. Dr. Michelle Bentley is not alone in testifying that activism cannot be divorced from faith. Her decades in community and parish ministry, as well as her work with the Central Midwest District and the UUA, is emblematic of this commitment. She relates the power of marching with Rev. Dr. Martin Luther King while a student at Spelman College in Atlanta and serving as an usher at his funeral service.

Melissa C. Jeter, a commissioned lay minister, listened to Rev. Dr. William J. Barber of the Poor People's Campaign speak at a UU society. He sparked hope in her heart and propelled her to seek a moral and mature faith in Unitarian Universalism. And Rev. Dr. Qiyamah Rahman stepped up when a category 5 hurricane devastated her home in the Virgin Islands. She birthed a nonprofit, Neighbor to Neighbor, which she views as the milestone in her ministry, calling forth "all that is whole, visionary, and prophetic."

Rahman is not alone in lifting up the gifts that come with ministry. The same voices that speak of discouragement, of hurdles, also describe blessings accompanying their calling. Sonya Tinsley-Hook liberates Pollyanna from saccharine distortions and instead reclaims her as the model of an approach Black women have used through generations to transform disheartening experiences.

Rev. Cheryl M. Walker's essay sheds insight into the often frustrating and lonely leadership journey of Black UU clergywomen. Her essay reminds us of the reasons so many of the women in this anthology honor their calls despite the obstacles.

So we Black Unitarian Universalist women continue on our journey. Sometimes our steps follow the footprints of those who have gone before. Other times we are on a solitary pilgrimage marked by snares. But we hold to a vision of ministry that welcomes all people—in our diversity, exquisiteness, and quest for a more just society.

So be it. Ashe. Ashe.

Chronology of Black Unitarian Universalist Clergy Women

This chronology was compiled at the end of 2020 from personal knowledge and Mark Morrison-Reed's *Darkening the Doorways: Black Trailblazers and Missed Opportunities in Unitarian Universalism* (Skinner House, 2011), colleagues, and Unitarian Universalist Association Directories.

Rev. Dr. Yvonne Seon, preliminary fellowship 1981, full fellowship 1988

Rev. Dr. Adele Smith-Penniman, preliminary fellowship 1982, full fellowship 1986

Rev. Dr. Michelle Bentley, preliminary fellowship (parish) 1986, full fellowship (parish) 1989, full fellowship (community) 1996

Rev. Toni Vincent, preliminary fellowship 1987

Rev. Marjorie Bowens-Wheatley, preliminary fellowship (parish) 1994, full fellowship (parish) 1997, preliminary fellowship (religious education) 2002

Rev. Dr. Thandeka, preliminary fellowship 1996, full fellowship 2002

Rev. Alma Faith Crawford, preliminary fellowship 1997

Rev. Dr. Kristen L. Harper, preliminary fellowship 1999, full fellowship 2002

Rev. Shana Lynngood, preliminary fellowship 1999, full
fellowship 2004

Rev. Rosemary Bray McNatt, preliminary fellowship 1999, full
fellowship 2004

Rev. Dr. Monica L. Cummings, preliminary fellowship 2000, full
fellowship 2006

Rev. Dr. Azande Sasa, preliminary fellowship 2002, full
fellowship 2015

Rev. Angela M. Davis, preliminary fellowship 2002

Rev. Dr. Hope Johnson, preliminary fellowship 2002, full
fellowship 2005

Rev. Janet Boykin Johnson, preliminary fellowship 2002

Rev. Dr. Rebekah A. Savage, preliminary fellowship 2002, full
fellowship 2012

Rev. Dr. Sofía Betancourt, preliminary fellowship 2003, full
fellowship 2006

Rev. Alicia R. Forde, preliminary fellowship 2004, full fellowship
2007

Rev. Addae Ama Kraba, preliminary fellowship 2004

Rev. Cheryl M. Walker, preliminary fellowship 2005, full
fellowship 2009

Rev. Joyce Palmer, preliminary fellowship 2006

Rev. Archene Turner, preliminary fellowship 2007, full fellowship
2010

Rev. Jacqueline Duhart, preliminary fellowship 2008, full
fellowship 2014

Rev. Dr. Qiyamah A. Rahman, preliminary fellowship 2008, full fellowship 2013

Rev. Karen Hutt, preliminary fellowship 2009, full felllowship 2013

Rev. Hafidha Fatou Saadiqah, preliminary fellowship 2009

Rev. Dr. Natalie Maxwell Fenimore, preliminary fellowship 2011, full fellowship 2015

Rev. Dr. Carol Thomas Cissel, preliminary fellowship 2013, full fellowship 2019

Rev. Patrice K. Curtis, preliminary fellowship 2014, full fellowship 2017

Rev. Lynnda White, preliminary fellowship 2014, full fellowship 2020

Rev. Kimberly Quinn Johnson, preliminary fellowship 2016

Rev. Jacqueline Brett, preliminary fellowship 2017, full fellowship 2021

Rev. Aisha Ansano, preliminary fellowship 2018

Rev. Sara Green, preliminary fellowship 2018, full fellowship 2022

Rev. Connie Simon, preliminary fellowship 2018, full fellowship 2021

Rev. Amanda Weatherspoon, preliminary fellowship 2018

Rev. Yadenee Hailu, preliminary fellowship 2019

Rev. Viola I. Abbitt, preliminary fellowship 2019, ordained 2020

Rev. Margalie Belizaire, preliminary fellowship 2020

I have tried diligently to identify all Black UU clergy women who have pursued ministerial formation but for various reasons did not achieve fellowship or sought fellowship elsewhere. Please contact Mary Benard, Publications Director at Skinner House Books, mbenard@uua.org, if you'd like to offer a correction or addition for a future printing of this book.

I acknowledge the following women for their presence, connections, and important contributions to Unitarian Universalism and specifically to ministry:

Rev. Joanne Braxton, Ph.D.

Rev. Dr. Denise Hall

Rev. Kimberly Rochelle Hampton

Rev. Dr. Susan Newman Moore

—QR

First Women of Color to be Fellowshipped and Ordained in Unitarian Universalism

Rev. Dianne Arakawa (Asian American), preliminary fellowship 1978, full fellowship 1984

Rev. Dr. Yvonne Seon (African American), preliminary fellowship 1981, full fellowship 1988

Rev. Dr. Danielle Di Bona (Indigenous), preliminary fellowship 1998, full fellowship 2003

Rev. Patricia Jimenez (Latina), preliminary fellowship 2018, full fellowship 2021

Ordination of Women Timeline

1853   Antoinette Brown Blackwell was ordained in the Congregational Church. She later fellowshipped with the Unitarians.

1863   Olympia Brown was ordained as the first Universalist woman minister.

1868   Meadville Theological School in Meadville, Pennsylvania, began admitting women. At this time, there were only four Universalist women ministers in America: Olympia Brown, Phebe Ann Hanaford, Augusta Jane Chapin, and Ruth Augusta Damon Tabor.

1871   Unitarians ordained their first woman minister, Celia Burleigh.

1873   Marmora DeVoe Moody became the first woman to graduate from Meadville Theological School in Meadville, Pennsylvania.

By 1890   There were 70 ordained Unitarian and Universalist women.

By 1910   There were 684 women working as ordained ministers in all denominations in the country.

By 1920   130 Unitarian and Universalist women had been ordained.

1959-1960   Only 3 women clergy served Universalist congregations.

1968   Only 21, or 2 percent, of UU ministers were women.

1978   57, or 6 percent, of the total 916 UU ministers were women.

1988   Out of a total of 1,108 UU ministers, 276, or 25 percent, were women.

1998   49 percent of all clergy active in UU ministry were women, that is 504 women among a total of 1,035 ministers.

1999   Women represented 51 percent, the majority, of total UU ministers.

About the Contributors

Rev. Dr. Michelle Bentley has served with distinction across Unitarian Universalism for nearly forty years. After working as an educator in Chicago, Rev. Bentley became the first Black woman to complete her Master of Divinity from Meadville Lombard Theological School, and she received her DMin from Chicago Theological School. She served First Unitarian Church of Chicago and All Souls Free Religious Fellowship in Chicago, and was called as Senior Minister of Third Unitarian Universalist Church of Chicago. Later, she became the first African American/Minister of Color Dean of Students and Faculty at Meadville Lombard. Rev. Bentley then became Director of Professional Development at the Unitarian Universalist Association, where she co-created Finding Our Way Home and the annual General Assembly gathering of women of color. In addition, she founded and directed the Sankofa Special Collection, a historical archive of people of color in Unitarian Universalism. Bentley's activism led her to write grants to serve as Chaplain to the BRASS Foundation and LaRabida Children's Hospital for the Chronically and Terminally Ill and as Expert Consultant for the Cook County Public Defender's Alternative Sentencing Program for Capital Criminal Cases.

Rev. Marjorie Bowens-Wheatley served as Director of Public Affairs for the Unitarian Universalist Service Committee, Program Officer for the Veatch Program, Affiliate and then Associate Minister at the Community Church of New York, District Extension Minister for the Metro New York District, and Field Consultant for the Unitarian

Universalist Association Department of Faith in Action. In 1999, she became Co-Interim Minister of the First Unitarian Universalist Church in Austin, Texas, with Rev. Clyde Grubbs, her husband, and in 2000 she took became the Adult Programs Director for Religious Education at the Unitarian Universalist Association. She served the Unitarian Universalist Church of Tampa, Florida, from 2003 to 2006. Rev. Bowens-Wheatley died of gallbladder cancer in December 2006.

Rev. Jacqueline Brett was called as Lead Minister of the Eno River Unitarian Universalist Fellowship (ERUUF) of Durham, North Carolina, in 2022. She has served in various roles at ERUUF since 2012, was ordained by the congregation in 2017, and has also worked on staff at the Unitarian Universalist Fellowship of Raleigh and Community Church of Chapel Hill. Rev. Brett earned an MDiv and an MA in Leadership Studies from Meadville Lombard Theological School. She serves the UU denomination as a member of the Ministerial Fellowship Committee and is on the Board of Trustees of the Unitarian Universalist Service Committee. Rev. Brett is a member of the Strategy Team for the local organization Durham CAN (Congregations, Associations, and Neighborhoods) and is a co-chair of its Clergy Caucus. Prior to ministry, Rev. Brett worked in corporate communications and public relations and was a national executive recruiter specializing in those fields.

Rev. Angela M. Davis held an MS from the National College of Education and an MDiv from Starr King School for the Ministry. She was a member of the Association for Clinical Pastoral Education and she worked for the AIDS Alliance in Concord, California, from 1995 to 1997. She was employed by the Unitarian Universalist Association as the AIDS Network Coordinator from 1995 to 1998. She was drawn to chaplaincy work and became active with the San Joaquin Sheriff's Department and served as a volunteer chaplain at the University of

California at Davis Medical Center. Rev. Davis was also a member of the Continental Board of the Unitarian Universalist Women's Federation from 1995 to 1998 and was on the Board of the First Unitarian Universalist Society of San Francisco from 1989 to 1991. She volunteered for the United States Coast Guard Auxiliary and for Volunteers in Service to America (VISTA). Rev. Davis died in 2003 from a blood infection.

Rev. Dr. Natalie Maxwell Fenimore is Lead Minister and Minister for Lifespan Religious Education at the Unitarian Universalist Congregation at Shelter Rock in Manhasset, New York. She has been a religious educator and parish minister in Unitarian Universalist congregations in Maryland and Virginia. She formally served as President of the Liberal Religious Educators Association, as Vice President of the Board of Trustees of Starr King School for the Ministry, and as a member of the Unitarian Universalist Association's Commission on Institutional Change. She currently serves on the Board of the Unitarian Universalist Ministers Association. Rev. Dr. Fenimore is the author of several Unitarian Universalist religious education curricula, Renaissance Modules, meditations, and readings. She is a contributing author in *Centering: Navigating Race, Authenticity, and Power in Ministry* and *Widening the Circle of Concern: Report of the UUA Commission on Institutional Change*. Her DMin area of study is Narrative Theology with an emphasis on Story and Faith Development for African American Unitarian Universalists.

Rev. Yadenee Hailu studied, interned, and ministered within the Unitarian Universalist Association from 2015 to 2021. She earned an MDiv from Phillips Theological Seminary in 2018.

Rev. Dr. Kristen L. Harper is the Minister of the Unitarian Church of Barnstable, Unitarian Universalist, where she has served for twenty years. Rev. Harper received her DMin from Meadville Lombard in 1999. She has served congregations in Lansing, Michigan; Chicago, Illinois; and Ormond Beach, Florida, and contributed a chapter to *Centering: Navigating Race, Authenticity, and Power in Ministry*. She is the author of *The Darkness Divine: A Loving Challenge to My Faith*.

Melissa C. Jeter is a seminarian at the Methodist Theological School in Ohio as well as a full-time librarian in Toledo, Ohio, and the student minister affiliated with First Unitarian Church of Toledo. She has served on the Social Justice Subcommittee of the City of Toledo Human Rights Commission. She has been employed or volunteered in Toledo nonprofit agencies working on housing, civil rights, and domestic violence.

Rev. Dr. Hope Johnson served as the Congregational Life Consultant for the Unitarian Universalist Association's Central East Region and the Southern Region. She specialized in conflict resolution and multicultural congregational development. She was also the former Minister of the Unitarian Universalist Congregation of Central Nassau, New York, where she served for fifteen years. Previously, she served as Minister of Spiritual Life and Director of Religious Education at the First Unitarian Church of Brooklyn. She was a Unitarian Universalist leader in several contexts, including the Appointments Committee and the Nominating Committee of the Unitarian Universalist Association, the Continental Good Offices Team of the Unitarian Universalist Ministers Association, and a number of positions with the Unitarian Universalist College of Social Justice. Rev. Johnson died in 2020.

Rev. Janet Boykin Johnson received an MA in Social Work from the University of Chicago in 1972. She worked as a social worker within the Chicago Public School System for eighteen years. She then went on to attend Starr King School for the Ministry and graduated with an MDiv in 2002. Rev. Johnson was ordained to the ministry in 2002 by the First Unitarian Society of Chicago, Illinois. Subsequently, she served as a chaplain to cancer patients at a hospital in Richmond, California. From 2004 to 2007, she worked in a private spiritual direction practice and as a part-time minister to the Mt. Diablo Church of Walnut Creek, California. She was called to serve as consulting minister to the Unitarian Universalist Church of Cortland, New York, in 2008, and served there until her retirement in 2013. Rev. Johnson was on the Board of Directors of the River Oaks Towne Houses Cooperative and was a member of Amnesty International. From 1975 to 1992, she served as host and program coordinator of Experiment in International Living. After moving to California, Rev. Johnson sat on several pastoral care hospital boards and co-managed a clothing store operated by the Chaplaincy for the Homeless. She died in 2015 at the age of seventy-two.

Rev. Addae Ama Kraba earned an MDiv from the Starr King School for the Ministry immediately after receiving a BS in Organizational Behavior from the University of San Francisco. She has published work in *She Is Everywhere! Vol. 2: An Anthology of Writing in Womanist/Feminist Spirituality; Lifting Our Voices: Readings in the Living Tradition; Voices from the Margins: An Anthology of Meditations;* and *Conversations with the Sacred: A Collection of Prayers.* She serves the Unitarian Universalist Church of New Braunfels, Texas. Prior to ministry, Rev. Kraba spent more than twenty years in the field of mental health. She has served at all levels in Unitarian Universalism, including as a member of the Committee for Antiracism, Anti-Oppression and Multiculturalism of the Unitarian Universalist Ministers Association; trustee on the Board of the Murray Grove Retreat and Conference Center; and Boardmember of the Joseph Priestly District while serving the First Unitarian Church of Philadelphia as community minister. Reverend Kraba was called to be present as Chaplain in New Orleans after Hurricane Katrina, and again for the Unitarian Universalist Church in Knoxville, Tennessee, after the shooting there.

Rev. Dr. Azande Sasa is a former Arabic linguist and an ordained Unitarian Universalist community minister. A Fulbright-Hays fellow and graduate of Harvard Divinity School, she served as a military chaplain for eleven years and deployed in support of Operation Iraqi Freedom. A lifetime devotee of writing, the spiritual arts, and contemplative living, Rev. Azande is a certified One Light Healing Touch Energy practitioner. Her writings are published in Black Renaissance/Renaissance Noir and the book *Angels: Divine Encounters with Beings of Light.* She is the author of the upcoming book *Interlife: Near Death Consciousness as the Key to Profound Living* under her *nom de plume*, Azande Mangeango.

Rev. Dr. Rebekah A. Savage serves the Unitarian Universalist Congregation of Rockville, Maryland. She holds an MDiv from Union Theological Seminary and has completed Clinical Pastoral Education at a large hospital in Miami and her internship at the Boca Raton Unitarian Universalist Congregation in Florida. Rev. Savage felt drawn to military chaplaincy after September 11, 2001, and was commissioned in 2003. Since then, she has spent the majority of her career on active duty and completed an overseas tour in Afghanistan. In 2007, she completed an MA in Mental Health Counseling and became a licensed professional counselor in 2014. In 2020, she completed her DMin in Military Chaplaincy at Wesley Theological Seminary. She also serves as the Co-chair of the Unitarian Universalist Association's Ministerial Fellowship Committee.

Rev. Dr. Yvonne Seon is the first Black woman ordained as a Unitarian Universalist minister. She is also the author of *Totem Games: Poems in Search of African Identity*. She was an administrative officer in the government of Patrice Lumumba in the Democratic Republic of Congo and also worked in the U.S. federal government. She then worked as a university administrator and founded a Black Studies Center at Wright State University and helped to design one of the first doctoral programs in Black Studies in the United States.

Rev. Connie Simon was called in 2018 as the first minister of color of the First Unitarian Church of Cincinnati. She held a variety of positions in government, law, business, and nonprofit management before answering the call to ministry. She is currently Secretary of the Unitarian Universalist Ministers Association, Board Member and Alumni Association President at Meadville Lombard Theological School, and an advisor for the Ministerial Formation Network. Deeply devoted to the study of Unitarian, Universalist, and Unitarian Universalist history and sharing the untold stories of BIPOC Unitarian Universalists, Rev. Simon is a member of the Board of the UU Studies Network and Editor of the Dictionary of Unitarian and Universalist Biography.

Rev. Dr. Adele Smith-Penniman is the first African American woman to receive final fellowship in the Unitarian Universalist Association and has worked in both community and parish settings with a deep commitment to marginalized communities. Her peace and justice activism dates back to 1960 and has included full-time work with SCLC and SNCC. She began her studies at Harvard Divinity School when women were re-envisioning theology. Bringing her long-standing commitment to feminism/womanism, she served on the National Council of Churches Commission on Women in Ministry, was Co-director of the Women's

Theological Center, and was Massachusetts Director of the national Religious Coalition for Reproductive Choice.

Sonya Tinsley-Hook has an MS in psychology and leadership and has had a variety of professional experiences, including directing an inner-city youth program, community organizing, and being a performing singer-songwriter. She is currently a strengths and career coach within a global professional services organization. Her activism and community service work has been featured in Paul Loeb's books *The Soul of a Citizen* and *The Impossible Will Take a Little While*. She is an active member of the Unitarian Universalist Congregation of Atlanta, where she has served as a lay minister since 2018 and sings regularly during services as a member of the Love Supremes vocal group.

Rev. Toni Vincent was a founding member of the Network of Black Unitarian Universalists and served as its president from 1985 to 1990. She also co-convened the African American Unitarian Universalist Ministry. She served as New Congregation Minister for New Community Congregation in San Francisco from 1991 to 1993 and as Minister to Sepulveda Unitarian Universalist Society in Mission Hills, California, from 2000 to 2002.

Rev. Cheryl M. Walker serves as the Interim Minister of the Unitarian Society of Germantown in Pennsylvania. She served as the Pastor of the Unitarian Universalist Congregation of Wilmington, Delaware, from 2009 to 2022. Before that, she served for four years as the Assistant Minister at the Unitarian Church of All Souls in New York City. Rev. Walker is a past President of the Unitarian Universalist Ministers Association. She has published essays in several Unitarian Universalist collections including, *Turning Point: Essays on a New Unitarian Universalism, Centering: Navigating Race, Authenticity and Power in Ministry,* and the *Unitarian Universalist Pocket Guide.* Rev. Walker holds a BA in Mathematics from Springfield College and an MDiv from Union Theological Seminary in New York.

Acknowledgments

I am grateful to the good in the Universe that conspired with me to make this anthology possible. I am grateful that I have been faithful to my ministry of writing and that I did not decline the call though writing can sometimes be a frustrating endeavor.

I acknowledge each of the contributors who said yes to my request and trusted me enough to believe that we could create something good together. Thank you for your trust.

To Rev. Dr. Mark Morrison-Reed, my writing mentor who, unbeknownst to him motivated me to conceive and birth this anthology. To my editing sista, Junee Hunt, who helped me get through some tough editing moments. To Dr. Nubia Kai, who identified the names of Biblical and African women for me and let me know that I was not off track. Thank you to Dr. Stephanie Mitchem for her extensive reading and editing.

I am grateful to Skinner House Books for their support. I also wish to acknowledge Africana Women's Studies at Clark Atlanta University, where I acquired and honed my research skills under the watchful eyes of Dr. Jacqueline Howard-Matthews. And to others, too numerous to name, who helped me along the way. And to those who did not contribute for various reasons, I understand and know that there will be other opportunities in the future for you to say yes.